TRUSTING GOD *in* TROUBLED TIMES

Developing UNSHAKABLE *Faith*

for UNPREDICTABLE *Circumstances*

R.B. Ouellette

First published in 2012 by Striving Together Publications, a
ministry of Lancaster Baptist Church, Lancaster, CA 93535.
Striving Together Publications is committed to providing
tried, trusted, and proven books that will further equip local
churches to carry out the Great Commission. Your comments
and suggestions are valued.

Striving Together Publications
4020 E. Lancaster Blvd.
Lancaster, CA 93535
800.201.7748

Cover design by Andrew Jones
Layout by Craig Parker
Edited by Robert Byers
Special thanks to our proofreaders

The author and publication team have given every effort
to give proper credit to quotes and thoughts that are
not original with the author. It is not our intent to claim
originality with any quote or thought that could not
readily be tied to an original source.

ISBN 978-1-59894-194-4
Printed in the United States of America

Dedication

To my sister, Beth Ouellette. Your consistent generosity, exceptional diligence, high integrity, and commitment to your family are an example and encouragement. I love you.

Contents

Acknowledgements

Once again, Robert Byers has done a masterful job of transcribing, editing, and improving my material. Your encouragement is responsible for my foray into the printed word. Thanks.

Brother Cary Schmidt and the staff at Striving Together Publications always impress me with their quality, creativity, and industry. Thanks for making this production so much better than it otherwise would have been.

I am undeservedly blessed with a tremendous wife, two wonderful daughters, two beloved sons-in-law, the world's best granddaughter and grandson, an excellent staff, and a great church family. Your love and support make my ministry possible and my life delightful.

Introduction

Some truth is temporary. For instance, when I came to the First Baptist Church of Bridgeport in 1975, I was referred to by many as a young pastor. When my dad was in college in the late 40s and early 50s, he was a great weightlifter. Many years ago, I bought a new car. Well, I'm still a pastor but the adjective "young" is never applied to me except in the negative sense. My dad, at the age of 84, is active but no longer a weightlifter. The new car wore out, rusted, and has been off the road for some time.

Much of the advice we receive from worldly sources is false and cannot be trusted. That which appears solid is often temporary. The prime neighborhood of this year may become a slum in a few decades. The hot stock of today may be a sub-par performer later this year. The champs of this season could end up the chumps of the next.

But some truth is timeless. It can be trusted. It is always accurate, valuable, useful, and helpful. Such are the truths of God's wonderful, inspired, inerrant, infallible, preserved, and perfect book—the Bible. They will work under any form of government, help us in any economy and stand through any storm.

It is some of these timeless truths that are the focus of this book. While particularly helpful in our current difficulties, they will be equally true in prosperity or in poverty, in turmoil or tranquility, whether we are living in a time of burden or in a time of blessing.

God's timeless truths are trustworthy. Whatever circumstances we are in, we can confidently trust God and anchor our faith in His dependable precepts.

May the Lord encourage each reader to both learn and live His timeless truths.

ONE

A Scriptural Perspective on Hard Times

And Noah builded an altar unto the Lord; *and took of every clean beast, and of every clean fowl, and offered burnt offerings on the altar. And the* Lord *smelled a sweet savour; and the* Lord *said in his heart, I will not again curse the ground any more for man's sake; for the imagination of man's heart is evil from his youth; neither will I again smite any more every thing living, as I have done. While the earth remaineth, seedtime and harvest, and cold and heat, and summer and winter, and day and night shall not cease.*—Genesis 8:20–22

Somebody said that an optimist is a man who gets married at the age of seventy-five and tries to find a house near a school. Another example of an optimist is a fellow who has three teenage children and one car. Someone else said an optimist is one who goes to a picnic with four pounds of steak, five pounds of charcoal and one match.

On the other end of the spectrum we have pessimists. These are the glass-half-empty people—the ones who will tell you all the reasons something won't work. I don't like to be a pessimist, although someone told me once that pessimists are the only people who have pleasant surprises!

Wherever you fall on the scale between optimism and pessimism, it isn't hard to notice that our society has suffered some reversals that have brought real and harmful effects on ordinary people. Unemployment has skyrocketed to the highest levels in nearly thirty years. The housing crisis, the stock market crisis, and various bubbles and scandals have shaken people's faith in our system. Most people have been affected to a degree by the downturn. What I want to do is give a scriptural perspective on the economic woes we have experienced.

THE PATTERN

Notice that the pattern of cycles is seen in Scripture. God declared the cycles of the seasons to Noah in our text. There is a season to plant and a season to harvest. There will be times of heat, and there will be times of cold. There will be times of light, and there will be times of darkness. God said these patterns will not stop as long as the earth remains.

We see this truth again in the story of Joseph in the book of Genesis. Pharaoh had his dream of the seven good cows and lean cows and the seven healthy ears of corn and withered ears of corn. Joseph correctly interpreted the dream as a warning from God that seven good and plentiful years would be followed by seven years of extreme famine. Because Pharaoh heeded the warning and placed Joseph in charge of preparing for the hard times to come, "much people" were saved from the famine.

This pattern of cycles is also one we see in our society. There are good years and bad years in the economy. The problem comes when we think the good times will last forever and the bad times will never come back. A person with that mindset does not properly prepare for the lean years during times of relative prosperity. Instead of waiting for the government to stimulate the economy, you can stimulate your savings account by spending less and keeping more.

Many people sank hundreds or even thousands of dollars into collectibles that were "hot" one day only to find themselves left with a box or bag of "treasures" that are worthless. Did you collect baseball cards? Beanie babies? Precious Moments figurines? My wife and I used to collect Precious Moments figurines. We didn't start doing it because of the value; I just saw one in a gift shop at an airport when I was heading home and thought Krisy would like it.

Over the years we accumulated several of them. We gave one to a pastor and his wife where I was preaching some years ago as a gift. After he had it for a while, he found it was retired, and they said it was worth seven hundred dollars! He put it back in the box it came in and put it away in the attic. It was too valuable to leave on the shelf and run the risk of it being knocked off and damaged. But Precious Moments pieces aren't worth that much now. In fact, today I think that particular figurine sells for about seventy dollars.

Things go through cycles. Back during the 1990s, the hottest thing was tech stocks. Everybody was talking about what they bought on NASDAQ. Then the tech bubble burst. More recently it's been real estate. When housing prices collapsed, it triggered a worldwide economic downturn. People who thought they were set for life because of their real estate investments found out they had nothing left—in fact many people went bankrupt because they owed more than they were worth.

If you have studied history, you may have heard of Tulip Mania. During the Dutch Golden Age in the early 1600s, tulip bulbs dramatically increased in value. According to some accounts, a single tulip bulb could bring in ten times the annual income of a skilled craftsman. In today's money that could equal as much as $500,000—for one bulb. People wanted them, and the supply was tightly controlled. But then suddenly the price collapsed almost overnight, and fortunes were lost. Throughout both Scripture and the history of society, we see these cycles of rising and falling prosperity.

THE PERSPECTIVE

Not long after the housing decline started, I was listening to the news which said that market conditions were the worst they had been in seventeen years. That sounded really bad until I stopped and thought about it. Seventeen years before then was the early 1990s. Times were tough then, but we started the biggest church building project we've ever done in 1991, and God provided for us. Things may be bad, but they are not hopeless.

I read about someone else who said we have the highest foreclosure rate since the Great Depression. Again, that sounds bad, but we need to keep things in perspective. Most of us don't remember the Great Depression. My dad was born in 1927, so he was two years old when the stock market crashed. The foreclosure rate then was 50%. Don't go past that too quickly—that means that half of everybody who had a mortgage was unable to pay it. By comparison, the state with the highest foreclosure rate in late 2009 was Nevada where one out of every 33 homes was in foreclosure. That's a pretty high rate, but it's a long way from 50%.

As of this writing, Michigan has the highest unemployment rate in the country. In early 2010, the unemployment rate reached 14.9%. That's bad, but it still means that 5 out of every 6 people who want to work have a job. During the Great Depression, unemployment was officially over 25%, and most economists think the real rate was closer to 33%. And it stayed there for years. The economy didn't fully recover until the Second World War. As we talk about tough times, we need to keep these facts in mind so that we don't lose our sense of perspective.

THE PRINCIPLE

Before I share a principle with you, it's important to understand this truth: if you understand the Bible and obey the Bible, you are much better equipped to deal with tough times than those who don't. Will things still be hard? Sure. You won't get a reduced gas or electric bill or mortgage payment just because you're saved. But by viewing life through the lens of Scripture, you improve your situation.

This principle is found in 1 Timothy 6:17–19. *"Charge them that are rich in this world, that they be not highminded, nor trust in uncertain riches, but in the living God, who giveth us richly all things to enjoy; That they do good, that they be rich in good works, ready to distribute, willing to communicate; Laying up in store for themselves a good foundation against the time to come, that they may lay hold on eternal life."* Now when we talk about those who are rich in this world, who are we talking about? We tend to think of being rich in terms of Bill Gates or Warren Buffett—the super rich. But compared to how the rest of the world lives, those of us in the United States (even during economic difficulty) are rich.

I will never forget the first time I crossed the border between the United States and Mexico. It was 1982. After I preached on Sunday night, I got in the car with Krisy and Pastor and Mrs. Tom Harrison, and we drove all the way to Midland, Texas. The next morning we drove across the border at Juarez. When we got across the border, I couldn't believe what I saw. There were people living in railroad cars. They made houses out of them. They made houses out of crooked sticks and corrugated metal for the roof. You could stick your hand right through the walls.

Little kids were trying to sell chewing gum or wash your windshield to get a little money. Keep in mind that Mexico isn't a third world country. It's a country with vast oil reserves and lots of natural resources. Yet in comparison to America, most of the people in Mexico are very poor. The food we'll throw away this week alone is better than the best meal millions of people will ever have in their entire lives. So the admonition Paul gives to Timothy applies to us.

It's easy to fall into the trap of trusting riches. When I have some money in my pocket, I feel good, and it's easy to be generous. If I have a few hundred dollars in my pocket and somebody needs something, I love to help them with their need. But if I get down to twenty or ten or five dollars, I don't feel so good. If I have a lot of money in my pocket I think, "Where do I want to go to eat?" If I don't have money and I get hungry, I think, "Oops. Better wait till I get home." When we think like that, we are demonstrating trust in uncertain riches.

One of the good things God wants to do for us in a time of crisis as we face in our nation today is remind us that none of it is forever. We do not enjoy our lifestyle courtesy of Uncle Sam, General Motors, the health care system, or anything else. No, we enjoy it because of God. He is the source of every good and perfect gift (James 1:17). And because He is the source and we are not trusting in riches, we should be willing to do good and find it easy to give to help others. There are three specific items Paul lays out for us as principles to govern the way we live in difficult days.

First, there is a fragile trust which is forbidden. Riches are not a valid source of trust or faith because they are uncertain. The danger comes when we have money and we think we're okay. You hear it everywhere in our culture—money makes the world go round, cash is king, whoever has the gold makes the rules. But God says, "No. I can wipe out all that in the snap of a finger. It can all be gone overnight." That is the point of the parable Jesus told of the rich fool. Even if you have "much goods laid up for many years," they are not a valid and lasting source of confidence. As we'll see later on, I believe it's wise to set aside money for the future. The Bible teaches this principle, but our trust should never be in worldly riches.

Second, there is a Father we can trust to be faithful. David said, "*I have been young, and now am old; yet have I not seen the righteous forsaken, nor his seed begging bread*" (Psalm 37:25). God has never failed to keep a promise He has made. Regardless of the situation you face, you can rely on Him to provide for your needs. There is no true or lasting security found in finances— but there is complete confidence in God. The point Paul is making is that we must place our trust in that which can truly be trusted, and that is never money.

Third, there is a future trust which is fruitful. God expects us to use the resources with which He blesses us to help others. He wants us to be rich, not just in material things but in good works. A number of years ago, a wealthy businessman donated $100,000 to build a church building. He was well off, and though it was a generous gift, it was not one that made him a pauper by any means. Some time went by, and his business went bad and he lost everything that he had. One day he and a friend walked by that church. The friend, who knew his story, said, "I bet you wish now that you hadn't given all your money to the church." The former rich man smiled and said, "No. If I had kept that money, I would have lost it too when I lost everything else." He pointed to the church and said, "That's the only thing I saved."

THE PROMISE

Our trust is grounded on the one thing that can never fail—the promises of the Word of God. The Bible says in Matthew 6:33, *"But seek ye first the kingdom of God, and his righteousness; and all these things shall be added unto you."* This is a promise that is not affected by changing circumstances or economic difficulty. You can count on it no matter what is happening around you in society.

In this verse we see **the priority**: that we must put God first. The first check you should write when you pay your bills is the tithe check. Proverbs 3:9 says, *"Honour the LORD with thy substance, and with the firstfruits of all thine increase."* I would sell my car and ride a bicycle before I would stop giving to God. I would make any adjustment necessary to make sure I obey God and put Him first with my resources. During the great famine in the days of Elijah, he went to the widow at Zarephath. He asked her to make him a meal before she fed herself and her son. And he made her the promise that, if she did, the little bit of food and oil she had would last throughout the famine. In faith she obeyed and put God first, and He honored the promise of the prophet and provided for her and her son.

We also see **the provider**: it is God who supplies our needs. The psalmist wrote, *"I will lift up mine eyes unto the hills, from whence cometh my help. My help cometh from the LORD, which* *made heaven and earth*" (Psalm 121:1–2). To a shepherd, the hills were a place that offered a wide array of resources. They offered grass where the sheep could graze during the heat of summer and water from the winter snowpack that would melt and run down to refill the streams and ponds. But notice carefully what he is saying; the hills are not the place to look for help—our help comes from the God who made the hills. When we put Him first, "all these things" are supplied for us.

THE POINTERS

Here are some practical pieces of advice to keep in mind as you navigate through hard times.

First, we need to be careful to whom we listen. Not everyone who is speaking confidently is giving you good advice. Some of the things I hear "financial experts" tell people leave me shaking my head. This is also true, though it should not be this way, in the spiritual realm. Not everyone who claims to be speaking for the Lord is actually speaking the truth.

> *For thus saith the* LORD *of hosts, the God of Israel; Let not your prophets and your diviners, that be in the midst of you, deceive you, neither hearken to your dreams which ye cause to be dreamed. For they prophesy falsely unto you in my name: I have not sent them, saith the* LORD.—JEREMIAH 29:8–9

In the George Samuel Clason classic *The Richest Man in Babylon*, Arkad learns a hard lesson when he loses his money because he trusted a brick-maker to go out and buy jewels for him. Because the brick-maker did not know the difference between real and fake jewels, he was deceived into buying worthless pieces of glass. Later Arkad is asked whether he trusts brick-makers. "About brick-making, they may give good advice," he replies. "Advice is given freely but should be looked upon skeptically," he goes on to tell his audience.

Second, we need to focus on what's really important. Troubled times can be painful, but they are temporary. Christians need to live for eternal things. The great missionary martyr Jim Elliot said, "He is no fool who gives what he cannot keep to gain what he cannot lose." I was in a hotel in Colorado on a preaching trip. I gave the maid a tract, and the next day I asked her if she had read it. When she said yes, I asked, "Did it make sense?" "Not really," she said. So I went through the plan of salvation with her, and she trusted Christ as her Saviour. That matters.

I wasn't worried about what the stock market did that day. I don't know if the bond market went up or down. Regardless of what happens to Fannie Mae and Freddie Mac, that lady is saved forever and will spend eternity in Heaven. Long after all the buildings on Earth have crumbled, the stocks and bonds have rotted away, and the financial institutions are only relics of history, her soul will live forever.

Third, we need to be careful. The Bible tells us to *"walk circumspectly"* (Ephesians 5:15). We need to be paying attention to what is going on around us—not in a worried or fearful manner, but being on guard so we are prepared to respond to what happens. *Keep some cash available if possible.* As the saying goes, "Cash is king." Having cash allows us to take advantage of opportunities for bargains. It also provides you with a cushion in case something happens.

One of the men in our church told me that his employer had a problem with their accounting and he didn't get his paycheck for a couple of weeks. I asked if he needed any money, and he told me he was fine. The next time I saw him, I asked how they were doing. He said, "Pastor, you told us a while back that we should work to build up three to four months of our income in a savings account, and we did what you said." I understand that not everyone is in a position to do that, but having some cash on hand will allow you to deal with a short-term problem without panic, worry, or frustration.

Be very cautious about adding debt. I don't believe that all debt is wrong in every situation, but it is always something to be careful about—now more than ever. For years I have advised the people in our church not to go into debt for depreciating items. Buying a washing machine or furniture or taking a vacation on credit is always a mistake. So many times I've heard people say, "I had to…," but it isn't true. We go into debt for these kinds of things because we want to. You can go to a laundromat; you can get a used couch at Goodwill; you can stay home and play ball in the back yard with your kids and not bear a crushing burden of debt.

Use a debit card instead of a credit card. It works the same, but it keeps you from spending more than you have. The first month you can't pay off your credit card balance in full, put it in a drawer and hide it. The second month you can't pay it off, cut it up into little pieces. Don't lightly add to your debt. However, because of the downturn there are also opportunities available. Some people who have their finances in order are finding this a great time to buy a house at greatly reduced prices. Just be very careful and cautious before adding debt.

Eliminate high interest debt as quickly as possible. Interest rates vary widely, and if you have the opportunity to transfer a credit card or other loan balance to a lower rate, you can save hundreds of dollars in payments over time. Some people are surprised to find that it is legal to pay more than the minimum payment every month. If you can get a lower interest rate, continuing to make the higher payment will pay off the balance faster.

In all that happens, remember this: the most important advice you will ever receive for any crisis, financial or otherwise, is to trust God. More than anything else we cover in this book, it is my hope and prayer that you will learn and remember that if you trust God and put Him first, He will take care of all your needs.

> *The LORD looketh from heaven; he beholdeth all the sons of men. From the place of his habitation he looketh upon all the inhabitants of the earth. He fashioneth their hearts alike; he considereth all their works. There is no king saved by the multitude of an host: a mighty man is not delivered by much strength. An horse is a vain thing for safety: neither shall he deliver any by his*

great strength. Behold, the eye of the Lord *is upon them that fear him, upon them that hope in his mercy; To deliver their soul from death, and to keep them alive in famine. Our soul waiteth for the* Lord: *he is our help and our shield. For our heart shall rejoice in him, because we have trusted in his holy name. Let thy mercy, O* Lord, *be upon us, according as we hope in thee.*
—Psalm 33:13–22

TWO

Making Spiritual Investments

Lay not up for yourselves treasures upon earth, where moth and rust doth corrupt, and where thieves break through and steal: But lay up for yourselves treasures in heaven, where neither moth nor rust doth corrupt, and where thieves do not break through nor steal: For where your treasure is, there will your heart be also. The light of the body is the eye: if therefore thine eye be single, thy whole body shall be full of light. But if thine eye be evil, thy whole body shall be full of darkness. If therefore the light that is in thee be darkness, how great is that darkness! No man can serve two masters: for either he will hate the one, and love the other; or else he will hold to the one, and despise the other. Ye cannot serve God and mammon. Therefore I say unto you, Take no thought for your life, what ye shall eat, or what ye shall drink; nor yet for your body, what ye shall put on. Is not the life more than meat, and *the body than raiment? Behold the fowls of the air: for they sow not, neither do they reap, nor gather into barns; yet your heavenly Father feedeth them. Are ye not much better than they? Which of you by taking thought can add one cubit unto his stature? And why take ye thought for raiment? Consider the lilies of the field, how they grow; they toil not, neither do they spin: And yet I say unto you, That even Solomon in all his glory was not arrayed like one of these. Wherefore, if God so clothe the grass of the field, which to day is, and to morrow is cast into the oven, shall he not much more clothe you, O ye of little faith? Therefore take no thought, saying, What shall we eat? or, What shall we drink? or, Wherewithal shall we be clothed? (For after all these things do the Gentiles seek:) for your heavenly Father knoweth that ye have need of all these things. But seek ye first the kingdom of God, and his righteousness; and all these things shall be added unto you. Take therefore no thought for the morrow: for the morrow shall take thought for the things of itself. Sufficient unto the day is the evil thereof.—*MATTHEW 6:19–34

It is very common for people to respond to difficult situations with fear. Over and over in the Scriptures we see admonitions to "fear not." In 2 Timothy 1:7 we are reminded that a spirit of fear does not come from God. Fear can cause us to turn our backs on God and try to devise our own solutions. We see this illustrated vividly in the life of King Ahaz of Judah. Second Chronicles 28 tells us that in his time of distress, Ahaz turned away from God and began sacrificing to the false gods of the Syrians. Ahaz even went so far as to take the gold and silver treasures out of the Temple for his own use. Fear can keep us from making the proper decisions; it can also keep us from making the proper spiritual investments. In this famous passage from the Sermon on the Mount, Jesus lays out for us some vital principles regarding how we handle and invest our money—not just in a temporal sense, but for eternity.

First, we see the priority of spiritual investment. Jesus instructed His followers to lay up treasures in Heaven. Understand that this command does not exclude the idea of earthly investment. We are expected to be good stewards of the opportunities and privileges God has entrusted to us. Proverbs 21:20 says, *"There is treasure to be desired and oil in the dwelling of the wise; but a foolish man spendeth it up."* Proverbs 13:22 says, *"A good man leaveth an inheritance to his children's children: and the wealth of the sinner is laid up for the just."* First Timothy 5:8 says, *"But if any provide not for his own, and specially for those of his own house, he hath denied the faith, and is worse than an infidel."*

The Bible is certainly not against earthly investment. In the parable of the talents in Matthew 25, the master returned to see what his servants had done with the money that he left in their care. When he came to the servant who buried his talent he said, *"Thou oughtest therefore to have put my money to the exchangers, and then at my coming I should have received mine own with usury* [interest]*"* (Matthew 25:27). Certainly the main thrust of that parable is that God wants us to take the talents, the abilities, and the opportunities He has given to us and produce spiritual progress for Him. But it is also a very fair application to say that

God expects us to take the material possessions that He gives us and increase them for His glory.

Our emphasis and primary focus should be on eternal investments. Jesus is telling us that whatever we have invested on Earth is insecure and temporary. Solomon warns us that *"riches certainly make themselves wings; they fly away as an eagle toward heaven"* (Proverbs 23:5). Millions of people found this to be painfully true over the past few years. Their investments in the stock market or in real estate proved to be fleeting and transitory. No matter how careful you are in selecting where to put your treasures on Earth, they are not permanent. The spiritual investments you make can never be stolen away or lose their value.

A few years ago I heard a story that illustrates this truth. A rich man died and went to Heaven. Because of his wealth, he had been accustomed to having the best of everything. As he gazed on the street of gold and the mansions, he grew excited. He had always had the biggest and best home in his neighborhood, and he couldn't wait to see where he would be living in Heaven. But instead of a glittering mansion, he was taken to a tiny cottage. "That's it?" he asked. "That's where I have to live?" "That's all we could build with the materials you sent," the angel guiding him replied. Now that's not exactly the way things work, but it is a reminder that the spiritual investments we make are the ones that produce eternal results.

The majority of our focus should be on the things that matter for eternity. Many years ago, George Truett was the pastor of the First Baptist Church in Dallas, which at the time was the largest church in the world, both in terms of membership and income. One of his members was a very wealthy rancher. When Truett visited his ranch, the man said, "Pastor, look that direction. As far as you can see, I own it. Look this direction. As far as you can see, I own it. Everything you can see from here belongs to me." He expected his pastor to be impressed, but George Truett simply pointed up and asked, "How much do you own in that direction?" What have you invested in eternity?

Second, we see the purpose of spiritual investment. God's work takes money. We have to send money to the missionaries so they can stay on the field. We have to pay the teachers in the Christian school. We have to print tracts to pass out to the lost and Sunday school material for our children. But while it takes money to do God's work, that is not the primary reason God wants us to give. We are to make spiritual investments because of the impact that it has on our hearts. Jesus said, *"For where your treasure is, there will your heart be also"* (Matthew 6:21).

The primary purpose of making spiritual investments is not to advance the harvest; it is to attach our hearts. Some people check the Dow Jones Average many times a day because that is where their treasure is. In the abstract there isn't much entertainment value in watching a bunch of numbers crawl across the bottom of a television screen, but their hearts follow their treasure. At the place where I work out, they have a television set by the exercise equipment. I was there one day and a guy on the treadmill was watching the NASDAQ quotes and he said, "Oh no, no, no. Don't go down any further!" Those declining numbers weren't bothering me at all—that isn't where my treasure is.

If we were making this observation, we would probably say it backwards—that where our heart is, there we will put our treasure. I think that there is some truth in that. I've heard people say, "You can give without loving, but you can't love without giving." God says we will love that to which we give. Notice that we are not told to love first and then give; we are told to give first, and then we will certainly love.

Third, we see a precaution about spiritual investment. At first glance the next couple of verses in Matthew 6 don't seem to be connected to the topic of money. We don't talk about light coming into our body through our eyes. We see light with our eyes. What Jesus means when He talks about the light of our body being the eye is that our perception is shaped by our focus. If our eye is single—if we have the primary goal and purpose in life of honoring and glorifying God—then everything we do will have focus and clarity.

Years ago, when we moved to our house on Moore Road, I quickly discovered that I wasn't going to enjoy using a push mower very much. I remember the first time I finished mowing the grass with the riding mower. When I looked back at my work, the lines were anything but straight. Someone told me the old farmers knew the trick of straight lines. Find an object in line with the direction you are going and keep looking at it until you reach the end of the row. If you maintain a singular focus, purpose, desire and goal, it keeps you from getting off track.

From time to time someone will ask me why I continue to stay and pastor in an area that has suffered such a devastating economic downturn and experienced such a decline. The answer to that question is found in the reason I came here in the first place. My eye wasn't on building the largest independent Baptist church in Michigan. My eye wasn't on an ever-increasing membership with accompanying growing offerings. My primary focus—then and now—is reaching people with the Gospel of Jesus Christ.

The truth is that Bridgeport-Flint-Saginaw probably isn't a very good place to build a business these days. Church growth experts wouldn't suggest this as a place to start a thriving congregation. However, the one thing we do have is a lot of sinners. No matter what the economy does, I don't think we're going to run out of sinners any time soon. As a result, despite the declining population and one of the highest unemployment rates in the country, our outreach ministries continue to thrive. We still have people coming to Reformers Unanimous and replacing their dependence on drugs and alcohol with a relationship with Jesus Christ. We still have children, teenagers, and adults riding the buses. God is doing marvelous things because our focus has stayed on seeing sinners saved.

Fourth, we see the protection of spiritual investment. Not long ago, Congress voted to raise the amount of money in bank accounts that was covered by the Federal Deposit Insurance Corporation from $100,000 to $250,000 per account. I can tell you that the change they made didn't affect me at all. I didn't sleep any better that night. God has a far better plan for protecting our investments than the government. The spiritual investments that we make are safe and secure. The source of that protection is God. The same God who ensures that the birds of the air are fed and the flowers of the field are arrayed beautifully knows everything we need, and He has promised to protect that which we entrust to His care.

If we could sit down and talk to first century Christians, they would be astonished by the things that worry us. Most of us have food for at least several days in our homes. Most of us have at least a little bit of money in the bank. Most of us decide what we will wear from a closet with many options in it. I believe that we have begun to regard luxuries as necessities because of the relative prosperity of our nation. We have fallen into the trap of assuming that our blessings are our birthrights. Jesus said that God would provide food and clothing for us, not that we would have everything we could ever imagine wanting.

It is far more convenient to have two cars than one, but it is not a necessity. I like to take a vacation now and then, and I think it is good and proper to do so, but it is not a necessity. I enjoy taking my wife out for a nice meal, but it is not a necessity. God has promised to protect and sustain us by meeting our needs. Yet too many of His children are pouting because they aren't abundantly wealthy.

In 1993, we moved into the house we currently live in. The property was originally about 30 acres, but our plan was to sell part of the land and keep the 10 acres we have now. During the process of selling the land, the Department of Natural Resources came out and said the site was polluted—no homes could be built on it, and we couldn't sell it. I had a mortgage on the property, and I knew we needed to sell that land or we would be in trouble financially. For a while it looked as if we might lose the house. Eventually the state took care of the pollution problem at no charge to us and everything worked out.

During those days when we didn't know what was going to happen, I remember thinking, "I'm glad it's a problem with the house instead of one of the girls." If we had lost the house, I would have been sad about it, but we would have found another place to live. We would have continued enjoying time together as a family, working in the church, and doing the work of God. Throughout that experience, I was reminded of the things that are really important. Life is not about stuff.

Finally, we see the promise of spiritual investment. I know some people whose main goal in life is to save and accumulate wealth. Some of them managed to acquire a lot of money only to lose it when the economy collapsed. That hasn't been my goal, and yet God has added many wonderful things to me. If you worry about God's business and let Him worry about yours, you will always end up ahead in the bargain.

We have had missionary Don Sisk in our church many times. He spent decades on the field in Japan and then served as the head of Baptist International Missions for several years. Dr. Sisk told me that on a few occasions he was mistaken for Sam Walton, the founder of Wal-Mart, while Mr. Walton was still alive. Dr. Sisk said that he imagined Sam Walton coming up to him and proposing that they go into business together. They would each contribute all of their resources and then share the proceeds 50–50. Would that be a good deal? Of course! They wouldn't have been investing the same amount, but they would have been sharing the rewards.

God's resources far surpass those of the richest people we can imagine. So why don't we seek God's kingdom first and take Him up on His offer to add "all these things" to us? The problem is that we don't believe God will come through for us. We don't believe the promise of spiritual investment even though we may pay lip service to it. The way to determine what we truly believe is by evaluating actions, not words. Put your faith into action and enter the great partnership with God that places Him in charge of what is added to your life according to His resources. Our ambition should be to please and honor Him and advance His cause. If we do, God will take care of all our needs.

THREE

What Controls Your Mind?

Be careful for nothing; but in every thing by prayer and supplication with thanksgiving let your requests be made known unto God. And the peace of God, which passeth all understanding, shall keep your hearts and minds through Christ Jesus. Finally, brethren, whatsoever things are true, whatsoever things are honest, whatsoever things are just, whatsoever things are pure, whatsoever things are lovely, whatsoever things are of good report; if there be any virtue, and if there be any praise, think on these things. Those things, which ye have both learned, and received, and heard, and seen in me, do: and the God of peace shall be with you.
—PHILIPPIANS 4:6–9

In 1895, Rudyard Kipling wrote a short poem inspired by an ill-fated British military raid against the Boers in South

Africa. When it was first published fifteen years later, it became an immediate favorite, and is still quoted often today. The poem is titled simply "If."

> *If you can keep your head when all about you*
> *Are losing theirs and blaming it on you,*
> *If you can trust yourself when all men doubt you,*
> *But make allowance for their doubting too;*
> *If you can wait and not be tired by waiting,*
> *Or being lied about, don't deal in lies,*
> *Or being hated, don't give way to hating,*
> *And yet don't look too good, nor talk too wise:*
>
> *If you can dream—and not make dreams your master;*
> *If you can think—and not make thoughts your aim;*
> *If you can meet with Triumph and Disaster*
> *And treat those two impostors just the same;*
> *If you can bear to hear the truth you've spoken*
> *Twisted by knaves to make a trap for fools,*
> *Or watch the things you gave your life to, broken,*
> *And stoop and build 'em up with worn-out tools:*
>
> *If you can make one heap of all your winnings*
> *And risk it on one turn of pitch-and-toss,*
> *And lose, and start again at your beginnings*
> *And never breathe a word about your loss;*
> *If you can force your heart and nerve and sinew*
> *To serve your turn long after they are gone,*
> *And so hold on when there is nothing in you*
> *Except the Will which says to them: "Hold on!"*

If you can talk with crowds and keep your virtue,
Or walk with kings—nor lose the common touch,
If neither foes nor loving friends can hurt you,
If all men count with you, but none too much;
If you can fill the unforgiving minute
With sixty seconds' worth of distance run,
Yours is the Earth and everything that's in it,
And—which is more—you'll be a Man, my son!

I love that poem because it so clearly expresses a great truth—don't be controlled by things around you; don't let your attitudes and actions be dictated by circumstances. Instead practice what the Word of God teaches about self-control. You are not responsible for every thought that comes into your head. But you are responsible to put out of your head all the thoughts that don't belong there. You can bring every thought into obedience to Christ (2 Corinthians 10:5).

We had a man in our church who lost his job. Now jobs are so plentiful in Michigan these days that it was no problem at all! Well, not exactly. In fact unemployment in Michigan remains one of the highest in the nation. I talked to him the week it happened, and he said, "It's going to be all right. God has a plan for us." I know that wasn't the only thought he had after he lost his job. It was, however, where he was keeping his focus. You can determine where your mind goes and what controls it. This is vitally important because what you think determines how you will feel and how you will act.

THE PROHIBITION

"Be careful for nothing"

We use the word *careful* in different ways. In the winter when the roads have ice on them, we tell people to drive carefully—meaning "to be cautious." But as it is used here, it means "to be worried or anxious; to be full of care." Dr. John R. Rice had a sermon that he preached from this passage called "God's Cure for Anxious Care." The Bible tells us here what not to think. We are exhorted not to be controlled by worry and care.

This prohibition is extensive. The Greek word translated *nothing* means "not even one, no, not at all." It is emphatic. It includes all the things we might possibly worry about. There aren't any exemptions or exceptions. The command is simple—don't worry. That's not an easy thing to do, but since it is commanded by God, we know it must be possible.

When I was taking driver's education back in high school, they taught us about steering. I'll never forget what the teacher said: "Aim high." He pointed out that most new drivers look too close to the hood of the car. If your attention is focused on what's right in front of you, you will miss things that are coming at you. Then he said, "You tend to drive where you look." If you look out the window at something, you will tend to start drifting in that direction.

Life is the same way. When we are focused on our worries, they grow and take over our minds. Why did Peter sink when he was walking on the water toward Jesus? Because he focused on the winds and the waves instead of the Lord. Don't allow yourself to be driven and dominated by worry. How can we keep from worry? We must replace it with something else.

THE PRAYER

"but in every thing by prayer and
supplication with thanksgiving let your
requests be made known unto God."

The only way to worry about nothing is to pray about everything. Each trial and trouble of life is to be met with prayer. Dr. Bill Rice had a radio program that promoted the work and ministry of the Bill Rice Ranch. One day on the program, he prayed for his dog when it was sick. A listener wrote in and complained that it wasn't proper to pray for a dog. Dr. Rice read that letter on the air and then said, "I wouldn't have a dog I couldn't pray for." God is concerned about every part of your life, and He both allows and instructs us to bring our prayers to Him about "every thing."

I have a list of things for which I pray regularly. I use the model prayer, what many people call the Lord's Prayer, as an outline for my praying. There are regular times when I pray. But there is also a Bible truth that we are to pray without ceasing (1 Thessalonians 5:17). The idea there is not *continuous* prayer but rather *continual* prayer. If you turn the faucet on and water flows in a steady stream, that is continuous. If you turn the faucet off and it drips every three seconds, that's continual. You will not always be praying, but you can and should be continually praying. You should never be too far between prayers.

Pour out your soul to God and come before Him with your petitions. We talk about "venting" when we get something off our chests. At Bob Jones University they had signs that read, "Griping not tolerated; constructive suggestions are appreciated." When you pour out your frustrations and troubles to God, you are talking to the one who can always do something about your situation. When we tell everyone around us about our problems, it tends to ingrain them in our minds. When we tell God, things change. God not only understands what you are feeling, but He can do something about it.

We see this principle of overcoming worry beautifully illustrated in the life of Daniel. You know the story—Daniel peacefully slept through the night even though he was in the den of lions. Why did Daniel sleep while the king tossed and turned all night long? Look at what the Scripture says.

> *Now when Daniel knew that the writing was signed, he went into his house; and his windows being open in his chamber toward Jerusalem, he kneeled upon his knees three times a day, and prayed, and gave thanks before his God, as he did aforetime. Then these men assembled, and found Daniel praying and making supplication before his God.*—DANIEL 6:10–11

THE PRAISE
"with thanksgiving"

This is the part that we so often miss. My friend Dr. Curtis Hutson had a sermon he preached called, "Thanksgiving in

Reverse." The idea was to start giving thanks even before the answer comes. Most people don't do that. As I counsel with people, I hear about a lot of problems. People are struggling in their marriage, people have lost their jobs, people are having trouble with their kids, people have received bad news from the doctor—I hear it all. How much thanksgiving do you think I hear in those sessions? Not much.

I've heard many wonderful testimonies of people giving thanks for the great things God has done for them. It's wonderful to praise God for what He has done, but we are also to praise Him for what He will do. Pray with thanksgiving. God knows what He is doing, and He loves you so much that He will see to it that you receive His best for your life. Thank Him for His goodness, even before you receive deliverance.

In *The Hiding Place,* Corrie ten Boom told the story of her time with her sister Betsie at the dreaded Ravensbruck death camp during the Holocaust. They were arrested for hiding Jews from the Gestapo and placed in the women's dorm at the prison. When they arrived, they found it was infested with fleas. Corrie was horrified, but her sister said they were to follow the Scripture *"In every thing give thanks"* (1 Thessalonians 5:18). Later they found out that because of the fleas the guards would not enter the room. They were able to conduct Bible studies and lead many women to the Lord because of what seemed like one more burden to bear.

Our oldest daughter, Karissa, was adopted. During the adoption process, we had some difficulties. The birth father changed his mind and decided he was going to contest the adoption. One day I was praying and pouring out my heart to God. (I hadn't quite gotten to the thanksgiving part yet!) I prayed something like this: "Lord, we've been married ten years and never had a child. We didn't complain; we accepted it as something from You. We took whatever You gave. Why would You bring this little girl into our lives and then take her away?"

While I was praying, the Spirit of God convicted me about the principle found in this passage. I had a wrong spirit. At that moment I realized that Karissa would be in our home as long as God wanted her there—and that was as good a guarantee as anyone could have. I began to pray with thanksgiving. That was in 1983. We ended up paying some $13,000 for the legal fees for the contested adoption. We had no money. We didn't own a home then. We owned nothing and owed nothing. We had to borrow the money—it took until she was five years old to pay it off.

The law was against us. The Supreme Court had ruled in another case that the rights of even a fugitive father had to be considered. We had a good judge who focused on the best interests of the child, and he ruled in our favor. Then, that ruling was appealed. We didn't know what was going to happen. But my praying had changed. Now I prayed something like this: "Lord, thank You that You put it on a preacher's heart to tell us about this little girl. Thank You that she has been in our home since she left the hospital. Thank You for the joy and laughter she has brought to our home. Thank You for Karissa."

I did not lose all my worry. There were still moments when I was anxious about how things would turn out. I can't tell you that I had no apprehension, but I can tell you that the peace of God overruled my thoughts. I prayed and gave thanks, and worry no longer controlled my mind. There is no other way to get the peace that is beyond understanding than to pray with thanksgiving.

THE PROTECTION

"And the peace of God, which passeth all understanding, shall keep your hearts and minds through Christ Jesus."

To the Jewish people, peace was vitally important. The standard greeting, still in use today in many places, is, "Shalom aleichem…aleichem shalom"—Peace be unto you…unto you be peace. *Shalom*, the Hebrew word for *peace* has three distinct meanings—safe, happy, and well. The Hebrews lived in a time of near-constant war. The threats they faced were not like the ones we know today where war is mostly fought in distant, far-off lands. The enemies of Israel often invaded the land and brought the war to people's homes. Peace was so valuable because peace was so rare. But the peace that God offers is so much more than just the peace that comes from comfort and security.

In John 14:27 Jesus said, *"Peace I leave with you, my peace I give unto you: not as the world giveth, give I unto you. Let not your heart be troubled, neither let it be afraid."* A peace that comes from being safe, happy, and well is understandable. It makes sense. The world understands how someone with a good life, a good job, two nice cars in the garage, some money in a retirement plan, and good health insurance is going to be able to enjoy life and praise God.

Sometimes God gives us the privilege of praising Him from that position and using the material abundance that He has provided to us to be a help and encouragement to His work and to other people. Yet other times there are people who don't have anything, and you see them still praising God. They're still happy, and they're still rejoicing—that is peace that passes understanding. God doesn't promise to give you comfortable circumstances so you can enjoy life; He promises that in spite of uncomfortable circumstances, He will give you peace.

When Paul says that peace will "keep" our hearts and minds, the word *keep* means "garrison." Garrison can be either a noun or a verb. A garrison can refer to a fortress or protected place, or to the soldiers who are on guard duty in a location. God says that when we obey Him by replacing our worry and anxious care with prayer, supplication, and thanksgiving, His peace will stand guard and forbid worry from re-entering our hearts and minds. The peace of God provides us protection that is beyond human understanding.

THE PURPOSE

"think on these things"

In addition to replacing worry with prayer and thanksgiving, we also need to focus on things that are positive. When our focus is on things that are true, honest, just, pure, lovely, of good report, virtuous, and praise-filled instead of our fears and concerns, we are controlling our minds in a godly manner. You determine what you think on. What we see here is sometimes referred to as the doctrine of replacement. You do not just take out the bad; you must replace it with something else. Jesus taught this truth very clearly.

> *When the unclean spirit is gone out of a man, he walketh through dry places, seeking rest, and findeth none. Then he saith, I will return into my house from whence I came out; and when he is come, he findeth it empty, swept, and garnished. Then goeth he, and taketh with himself seven other spirits more wicked than himself, and they enter in and dwell there: and the last state of that man is worse than the first. Even so shall it be also unto this wicked generation.*—MATTHEW 12:43–45

Are your thoughts focused on things that are positive and uplifting? As a young pastor, I learned there are always good and bad things going on in the church. I learned that there is always someone who is unhappy and someone who is happy. There will be areas where things are moving forward and others where things are moving backward. I decided I would pray for the folks that were in trouble and help them if I could, but I would spend most of my time thinking about the good things that God was doing.

When I control my thoughts, I guard my heart. You can always find something to be discouraged about if you look hard enough. However, it's far better to look on the bright side. One of President Reagan's favorite jokes was about a little boy who wanted a pony for his birthday. When his father took him to a farm, he saw a huge pile of manure. The boy started jumping up and down. "Why are you so happy?" his father asked. "With a pile of manure that big, there has to be a pony!" the boy replied.

THE PROCLAMATION

"Those things which ye have both learned, and received, and heard, and seen in me, do"

Paul is reminding the Christians at Philippi of the things he had taught them. Notice that Paul both told and demonstrated for the people how they should live as followers of Jesus Christ. They had both "heard" and "seen" the truth from Paul. By his life and his lips, he had shown them what to do. If you hold any position of leadership—parent, pastor, Sunday school teacher, bus worker—you need to include both kinds of teaching. God has given you the obligation not only to know the truth but also to live it.

Dr. Tony Hutson today pastors a church, but when he was younger, he was a typical teenage boy. Once he came in and did something his mother didn't like. She said to her husband, "I don't know why he does that. I taught him better than that." Dr. Curtis Hutson replied, "You didn't *teach* him; you *told* him. If you had taught him, he wouldn't do that!"

Internalized truth is the only kind of truth that changes lives. No matter how much you teach and proclaim the truth, it is the truth that is "in me," as Paul said, that determines behavior. When we bring the doctrine of the Word of God into our hearts, it changes our conduct. And when we follow God's pattern for our thinking, we have His presence and peace in our lives.

Notice too that we must "do" those things. Jesus taught this truth in the Sermon on the Mount with the story of the wise builder and the foolish builder. What we know does not produce results; it is only what we do that protects us from the coming storms (Matthew 7:25–26). Knowing that prayer with thanksgiving can overcome worry doesn't bring peace. We must obey the instructions.

THE PRODUCT

"and the God of peace shall be with you."

It's wonderful to have the peace of God, but it's even better to have the God of peace. When He is with us, we have nothing to fear. A. B. Simpson, the founder of the Christian and Missionary Alliance, wrote a great old hymn called "Once It Was the Blessing" that beautifully illustrates this principle:

> *Once it was the blessing, Now it is the Lord;*
> > *Once it was the feeling, Now it is His Word;*
> *Once His gift I wanted, Now, the Giver own;*
> > *Once I sought for healing, Now Himself alone.*
> *All in all forever, Only Christ I'll sing;*
> > *Everything is in Christ, And Christ is everything.*

Once 'twas busy planning, Now 'tis trustful prayer;
  Once 'twas anxious caring, Now He has the care;
Once 'twas what I wanted, Now what Jesus says;
  Once 'twas constant asking, Now 'tis ceaseless praise.
All in all forever, Only Christ I'll sing;
  Everything is in Christ, And Christ is everything.

The Christian life is not mostly about what we get from God, though He gives good things to us freely; the Christian life is that we *get* God. Do you remember the story of Jesus crossing the lake at night with His disciples? While He was sleeping, a great storm came up—a storm so severe that even seasoned fishermen feared for their lives. When they woke Jesus, He rebuked them for their lack of faith. His presence should have been all they needed to have peace.

> *Thus saith the LORD, Let not the wise man glory in his wisdom, neither let the mighty man glory in his might, let not the rich man glory in his riches: But let him that glorieth glory in this, that he understandeth and knoweth me, that I am the LORD which exercise lovingkindness, judgment, and righteousness, in the earth: for in these things I delight, saith the LORD.*
> —JEREMIAH 9:23–24

I read about a good and godly man who worked for a nominally Christian school. (Not all those who claim to be Christians act that way!) During a power struggle, through no fault of his own, he lost his job. A friend came to commiserate with him. "I'll be all right," the man said. "After all, I have known God, and they have not." He recognized that the presence of God in his life was all that he really needed.

You can know, on a personal and intimate basis, the very God of Heaven. As you replace worry with prayer, supplication, and thanksgiving; as you focus your thinking on good, lovely, and true things; and as you take the things you have been taught and then internalize and do them, you will find Him a real presence in your life. If you keep all of your possessions but lose God, you will be in real trouble. If you lose all of your possessions but keep God, you will be just fine.

FOUR

Be Thankful in the Storms

But not long after there arose against it a tempestuous wind, called Euroclydon. And when the ship was caught, and could not bear up into the wind, we let her drive. And running under a certain island which is called Clauda, we had much work to come by the boat: Which when they had taken up, they used helps, undergirding the ship; and, fearing lest they should fall into the quicksands, strake sail, and so were driven. And we being exceedingly tossed with a tempest, the next day they lightened the ship; And the third day we cast out with our own hands the tackling of the ship. And when neither sun nor stars in many days appeared, and no small tempest lay on us, all hope that we should be saved was then taken away. But after long abstinence Paul stood forth in the midst of them, and said, Sirs, ye should have hearkened unto me, and not have loosed from Crete, and to have gained this harm and loss. And now

*I exhort you to be of good cheer: for there shall be no loss of any
man's life among you, but of the ship.*—ACTS 27:14–22

All of us from time to time go through storms in our
lives. While we may think it would be nice to live a life without
storms, in reality, we need them. Perhaps you remember the
large-scale science experiment called the Biosphere 2 from the
early 1990s. A series of glass enclosures were created to mimic
various climates and conditions in different parts of the earth.
A team of scientists lived sealed inside the structure for a time.
There were many unexpected results of the experiment, one of
which was that most of the trees did not do well. The trees were
very weak because they did not produce "stress wood"—the
hard buildup that trees produce in response to pressure from
the wind. The truth is that we need the storms. They help us
grow and develop as Christians.

In Acts 27 we see the story of a major storm in the life of the
Apostle Paul. Unlike his previous missionary travels to win souls
and start churches, this journey was taking him to Rome. There
he would be held in the Mamertine Prison. I've been to Rome
and visited that prison. It was home to notorious prisoners; it
would be home to Paul for several years. From his cell he would
write many of the books of the New Testament. Eventually he
would be taken from prison and martyred. The account of this
storm, and especially Paul's reaction to it, has some wonderful
lessons for us in dealing with troubled times.

THE CAPTIVITY

Paul had appealed to stand before Caesar, his right as a Roman citizen (Acts 25:9–12) because the Jews were waiting to kill him if he returned to Jerusalem. He had been arrested after a riot broke out when he visited the Temple. First Felix and then Festus had refused to release Paul, even though he had broken no laws. This journey was not the Mediterranean pleasure cruise that people take today; this was a prison ship taking Paul to judgment in Rome.

Paul was restricted on this voyage. He, along with a number of other prisoners, was in the custody of a Roman centurion named Julius. He did not have freedom to come and go as he pleased. There was no ACLU in those days to hector the government about their treatment of prisoners. Being in custody en route to Rome was no guarantee of kind treatment.

Yet despite his status, Paul was also respected. Julius treated him with courtesy. We should also live in such a way that even those who may not like our beliefs will respect the way that we live and interact with them. When they reached Sidon, Paul was permitted to visit with friends; the Bible says he was allowed to "refresh himself" (Acts 27:3). I'm sure that was a bittersweet meeting. Though they were glad to see Paul, these friends probably realized that they would never see him again.

THE CAUTION

At different times of the year, storms were more likely than others, and they had arrived at a time of year when it was risky to launch their journey. Because of his years of travel, Paul was very knowledgeable about weather conditions. Paul knew that because it was so late in the year, they faced great danger if they set sail. Of course such advice from a prisoner could easily be dismissed as a stalling tactic. Therefore, the centurion listened to the ship owner who told him what he wanted to hear rather than heeding the wise caution Paul offered.

In addition to the weather, the port where they were staying was not a good place to spend the winter, and I'm sure that also played into the decision to leave. Paul had declared that there was going to be trouble on the trip. It is normal for us to refuse advice that keeps us from doing what we want to do, and that is the course Julius chose. He listened to Paul, but he believed the owner of the ship more than what Paul said. It was not unreasonable for him to make that choice, but he was wrong.

A few years ago, I went to Mexico City to preach in a conference for pastors and church workers. I had been to Mexico many times, but it was my first visit to the capital. The host pastor left a note in my hotel room that read in part, "Don't go across the street to Wal-Mart by yourself. If you do, you are likely to be robbed, kidnapped, or killed." Now when you receive a warning like that from someone who has experience to back it up, you can choose to ignore it, but that may not be the wisest course of action to take.

Many times in life, where you end up is determined by whose advice you choose to follow. It's a question of who you believe more. Faith is not the complete absence of doubt and fear; it is believing God more than you believe your doubts. The father of the demon possessed boy said to Jesus, *"Lord, I believe; help thou mine unbelief"* (Mark 9:24). When you aren't sure what to do, believe God more than what you see with your own eyes. Believe the Bible more than you believe the counsel you receive from the world.

There are many roads that can lead us into storms. Some storms are the result of disobedience and unwise choices. Some of them are the result of living in a fallen world. Some of them are a part of God's refining process for our lives. Regardless of how we end up in the storm, it is a time of chaos when our faith is tested. Remember this, it is not the storm itself but rather our response to it that determines the outcome.

THE CHAOS

It's interesting that the chaos didn't start immediately. At the beginning of the trip, the winds were favorable, and the seas were calm (Acts 27:13). So many times we make the mistake of thinking that soft winds and smooth sailing guarantee we're on the right track. I've had people tell me, "Preacher, I know I should be doing that, but things are going okay." The fact that God is merciful and doesn't always immediately punish sin does not mean that He condones wrongdoing. Notice that it wasn't long until a furious storm arose and plunged the ship into chaos.

The Bible says the wind was called Euroclydon, which is the equivalent of what today we would call a "nor'easter." It was a great storm, probably close to hurricane-strength winds, that produced mighty waves and hid the sun and stars for many days and nights. That meant they had no way of knowing where they were. They had no control over the ship—it was forced to go wherever the wind took it. All they were doing was trying to survive. For fourteen days they struggled in the grip of the mighty storm until they reached the point where they gave up all hope.

There were 276 people on that ship—soldiers, sailors, and prisoners—and 275 of them were in despair. While the storm was still raging and they had no means of controlling either their direction or their destination, Paul stood up and said something amazing: "Be of good cheer." The message didn't seem to fit the circumstances. Imagine walking out of the doctor's office having just been told you have terminal cancer, and someone tells you, "Cheer up!" How would you respond? Imagine getting a notice by email that you've lost your job, and your coworker says, "Cheer up!" What would you say?

If someone who isn't going through the same struggle and storm you are says "Cheer up," you probably will not respond well. But Paul was just as much at risk as everyone else on the ship. He was literally in the same boat with them. Despite the storm, the wind, the waves, and the lack of hope, Paul said, "Cheer up." He had the same reasons to despair that they had, but he had an additional resource—he had been talking to God.

Paul did remind them that he had advised against making the trip. I don't think he was having an I-told-you-so moment. I sometimes say to people when they are embarking on a course of action that I think is unscriptural or unwise, "I hope I'm wrong. I hope things don't work out the way I think they will.

But you asked my opinion, and I have to tell you that I think you're headed for disaster. If things don't go well, please don't feel like I'm going to hold this over your head. I'll try to help you put the pieces back together."

I think Paul was trying to make sure they listened this time by reminding them of the past. He then gave them the reason for cheer—that no one on the ship would lose his life. Again Paul was telling them something that didn't square with their observation. These people had given up all hope. There was no human reasoning that supported what Paul was telling them. They had no other interest than survival. They didn't care about the cargo or getting to Rome or what would happen to the ship. Paul told them that there was hope where they saw none.

THE CONFIDENCE

How was Paul able to confidently declare that good news in the face of all available evidence? First, because of his position. He said, *"For there stood by me this night the angel of God, whose I am, and whom I serve"* (Acts 27:23). Because Paul knew he belonged to God and served Him, he was confident in God's promises. Second, because of the angel's presence. The angel standing beside him gave Paul a vivid sign of God's protection over His servant. God knew exactly where they were, even though they were hopelessly lost. Finally, Paul was confident because of God's purpose. The angel explained to Paul that God had a plan for him to go before Caesar.

Nothing—no storm, no enemy, no wild animal—could stop Paul before he accomplished what God had planned for him to do. When the great pioneer missionary John Paton was preparing to leave Scotland for the South Sea Islands, an old preacher told him, "Surely you will be eaten by cannibals." Paton replied, "After I die, my body will be eaten by worms anyhow. Eaten by cannibals or eaten by worms; it makes no difference to me." Just before he died at the age of 83, Paton wrote, "I claimed Aniwa for Jesus, and by the grace of God Aniwa now worships at the Saviour's feet." You are immortal until God is done with you. No one can take your life. You will not die until it is God's time. Obey God and let Him take care of everything else.

Paul not only told them they would survive, but he also encouraged them with his faith. If they had none of their own, they could rely on Paul's faith. He said, "I believe God." Your faith can be a powerful influence to help others do right. When the storms are raging, it's good to have people of faith around to encourage and help you—and you should do the same for others. You can believe God when the storm is raging. No matter how bad the economy gets, no matter how bad the environment gets, no matter how bad the political situation gets, no matter how much the morals of our nation decline, believe God. He is Sovereign. He rules and reigns over everything.

THE COWARDICE

Someone once said that storms don't make our character; they reveal it. The storm that drove Paul's ship showed the sailors to be cowards. They were the professionals. They were the ones who knew how to respond to situations and handle the ship. At the moment Paul had given them the assurance that they would survive, they decided to abandon the soldiers, prisoners, and other passengers to their fate and take care of only themselves. They planned to leave their responsibilities despite the effect it would have on the others.

The consequences of their actions would have meant nothing to them. They were trying to run away. Sometimes God wants to use us to help others in the storm, but we choose to run away. It's too difficult, too messy, too demanding, too costly. It's easier to wash our hands and run away. Some fathers and husbands decide they aren't getting what they want from their families and decide to find something or someone else. They abandon the wives they promised to cleave to until death and the kids who are looking to them for love and leadership.

Not only do we try to run before a storm, but we also run away from God during the storms. When things don't go the way we think they should, we blame God for the problem rather than realizing that He is our shelter in the storm and our only source of hope. Some drop out of church. Some stop reading the Bible. Others cut themselves off from Christian friends. But it is in the storm that we should run to God. *"The name of the LORD is a strong tower: the righteous runneth into it, and is safe"* (Proverbs 18:10).

I've been at First Baptist Church of Bridgeport for more than thirty-seven years now. Things have not always been perfect. Some days weren't much fun. People have gotten angry with me (that's hard to believe, I know) and caused trouble. The economy in our area has been tough. Many people have lost their jobs and moved away. I didn't stay because there were no storms; I stayed because it was the will of God. When the storm comes, you need to stay on the ship. It is important to your safety and the safety of others that you do not give up.

The soldiers didn't show good character either. After Paul warned them and they stopped the sailors from leaving the ship, the soldiers decided to kill all the prisoners. A Roman soldier who failed to guard a prisoner and allowed him to escape would forfeit his own life. However, they could deliver their prisoners either dead or alive without getting into trouble. They knew there was a good possibility that in the shipwreck and the storm, some of the prisoners might swim off and escape. Rather than taking on the risk themselves, they were willing to kill all the prisoners, even those who were not worthy of death.

THE COMPASSION

Despite the fact that he would never have been in that mess in the first place if they had listened to him, Paul cared about the condition of his shipmates. He realized that they had been under such pressure that they hadn't eaten, and so he told them to stop long enough to have a meal. They would need their strength to make their way to shore after the coming shipwreck. Notice also that even surrounded by those pagan people who wanted to kill him, Paul stopped and gave a public prayer of thanks for the food before they ate (Acts 27:35). As a result, they were happier;

Paul's confidence was infectious and influenced everyone on the ship for the better.

One person can make a huge difference. While on a visit to the Reagan Presidential Library in California, I watched the film of Reagan's speech in Berlin in 1987 when he said, "Mr. Gorbachev, tear down this wall!" Almost everyone in the administration hated that line in the speech. The State Department and the National Security Advisor told President Reagan he should take it out. But a young speechwriter named Peter Robinson had put it into the draft of the speech after spending time in Berlin and talking to the local people about their feelings regarding the wall. President Reagan overruled his advisers and kept the line in the speech. Four years later, the wall came down! Today one section of that wall is on display at the Reagan Library.

Your job is to shine as a light to the world—even, and perhaps especially, during the storms. I heard about a lady who went to talk to her pastor. She said, "I think I need to quit my job. It's a horrible place. The people don't do right, and they're so ungodly." The pastor asked her, "Where do people put lights?" "In dark places," she replied. If it's really dark, even a small light shines brightly. In hard times it's not our job to feel sorry for ourselves, to moan and groan, to complain about how unfair things are. It is our job to stand and say, "Be of good cheer. I believe God."

As Paul showed compassion to others, the centurion Julius showed compassion to Paul. When the soldiers wanted to kill the prisoners, he stepped in. He was willing to risk his own life rather than allow Paul to be killed. I think he realized the debt he owed Paul, first for the advice that would have prevented them from being in trouble in the first place, then for the prayers that had moved God to save their lives, and finally for the warning that kept the sailors from fleeing the ship. He showed compassion even at a great potential cost to himself.

THE COMPLETION

There's an old story about a man who had tremendous trust in God. Flood warnings were issued for his neighborhood, but he refused to leave. "God will deliver me," he said. As the water started to rise, a boat came by, and they urged him to get in. "No, God will deliver me," he said. The water continued to rise, and he climbed up to his roof. A helicopter came by and lowered a basket for him to get in. "No, God will deliver me," he said. He drowned. When he got to Heaven, he complained to God. "I trusted You. Why didn't You deliver me?" God replied, "I sent a boat and a helicopter. What else did you want?"

Now that's not a true story, but it does highlight a truth— while we do not work and walk in our own strength, God does expect us to do what we can do. Those on the ship who could swim went first, and those who could not found pieces of boards to keep them from drowning while they made their way to shore. God is able to work miracles, and I've seen Him do it. But sometimes we sit back and wait for miracles when we should be doing our part. In 1 Corinthians 3:9 Paul wrote, *"We are labourers together with God."*

Soulwinning is a great illustration of this truth. I cannot convict anyone of sin. I cannot forgive anyone of sin. I cannot save anyone. God does all that. However, I am responsible to witness, to pass out tracts, to call men and women to repentance, and to preach the Gospel to every creature. God will not do the things we cannot do until we do the things we can.

If you are in a storm and the boat is sinking and you can swim, jump in the water and start paddling. Do what you can to solve the problem. If God has enabled and equipped you to do something, do it! We would like the boat and the helicopter—the easy way out—but often God knows that we need the growth and development that comes from swimming all the way to shore. If you are not obeying God in the areas where you already know what to do (for example, reading the Bible, praying, attending church, witnessing and tithing), you are not swimming. Don't let those things go because of the storms.

Notice that some people couldn't swim. God didn't leave them out. There are times when you are doing everything you know to do and you're still sinking. Some of the people on Paul's ship found boards, others had only a broken piece of the ship to use, but all of them made it to shore. God will never leave you or forsake you. Whether you're a swimmer or a floater, don't lose your faith. God is able—He will keep you safe.

Before they left on the voyage, Paul warned them that the trip would cause "much damage" to the ship, the cargo, and even to their lives (Acts 27:10). Yet after Paul's long prayer and fasting, God delivered all of their lives. The news got better as the storm got worse. Sometimes God doesn't give us all of the judgment we could receive. Sometimes His mercy steps in and delivers us from what we deserve. Psalm 103:10 says, *"He hath not dealt with us after our sins; nor rewarded us according to our iniquities."* Don't ever hesitate to turn to God and beg for mercy. Let me share with you some observations about surviving the storms from this story.

THE CONCLUSIONS

Spiritual advice is always more valuable than secular advice. The world is filled with advice that sounds good to human wisdom but goes against Scripture. If you follow that advice, you increase your chances of ending up in a storm. If the centurion had listened to Paul instead of the owner of the ship, he would have had a much easier trip to Rome. The temptation is to listen to "experts" instead of someone who is speaking truth from the Word of God. Psalm 1:1 warns us of the dangers of walking *"in the counsel of the ungodly."*

If you go to a secular financial adviser, he will almost certainly tell you that you can't afford to tithe. It doesn't make sense to worldly wisdom to give money to God's work when you have bills piled up that you can't pay. He is giving you sound advice—if you leave God out of the equation. But if you follow that advice, you will forfeit the blessing that comes from obedience.

Decisions based on circumstances don't necessarily make for smooth sailing. The things we can see are very limited. The most important thing is to be in the will of God, not to choose the path that seems to provide the easiest course. In difficult times, the most important decisions are not financial, they are spiritual. Base your choices on the Word and will of God.

Stuff is not as important as life. When the storm was at its worst, the crew threw the cargo overboard in order to lighten the ship and increase their chances of survival. On her deathbed, Queen Elizabeth I reportedly said, "All my possessions for a moment of time." I'm not opposed to having stuff. I don't believe being a Christian requires a vow of poverty. I am opposed to stuff having you. Jesus said, *"...a man's life consisteth not in the abundance of the things which he possesseth"* (Luke 12:15). Sometimes God uses storms to remind us of what really matters and how much we need Him.

God knows exactly where you are. The ship was hopelessly lost. They hadn't seen the sun or stars for days. Their navigation equipment was worthless. They didn't have a GPS to say, "Turn left in three hundred yards." Yet when God sent an angel to stand beside Paul, He knew exactly where to have the angel go. He knows exactly what you need. He knows the burdens you can bear. Even when you are completely in the dark about what to do, God knows.

It is a blessing to suffer for Jesus. Paul told his shipmates to be of good cheer, that their lives would be spared and they would reach Rome. That was somewhat of a mixed blessing for Paul. He was headed to a jail cell. Later, he would appear before Nero and die for his faith. But Paul was willing to endure that because God had told him he would have the opportunity to preach the Gospel in Caesar's household. Paul was focused on fulfilling God's will for his life. He was willing to suffer and die for the sake of the Gospel.

Our attitude should not be based on our circumstances, but on God's promises. That's a simple statement, but it's hard to remember during the storms. It doesn't matter what the stock market does. It doesn't matter what the economy does. It doesn't matter what the news says. You will be okay because you belong to God. The storm didn't stop when God promised Paul that everyone on the ship would survive. They still had to go through the shipwreck. But because all God's promises are certain and true, Paul told the people to be of good cheer—even before things got better.

Any time is a good time to give thanks. The storm was howling. They were getting ready to eat one more meal before throwing all the rest of the food supply overboard also. And Paul stood up and gave thanks to God. You don't have to wait until the storm is over to be thankful. In fact you shouldn't. Being thankful is always God's will for your life (1 Thessalonians 5:18). Despite the circumstances, God is still there, and He is working all things together for your good.

God expects you to do what you can, even in a storm. Sometimes we act as if God owes us a free pass because of the storm. If you don't have a job, spend eight hours a day looking for a job. Sitting back and waiting for someone to call you is a recipe for failure. As we saw earlier, if you can swim, God expects you to swim. The responsibility you have doesn't go away just because some things aren't going right.

Don't complain about your means of deliverance. Making it to shore on a broken piece of ship isn't luxurious transport, but it beats drowning. God may use a method you don't expect. He sent dirty, scavenging ravens to feed Elijah during the drought. He had Naaman dip in the muddy Jordan River to be cleansed of leprosy. Quit looking around at what other people have and focus on hanging on to what God gave you.

Life's problems can never keep you from God's purpose unless you let them. The people on the ship viewed it as their security. They wanted it to hold together. But it was the destruction of the ship that provided those who could not swim with the boards they used to survive their trip to shore. Sometimes the things that seem the worst to us are the very instruments God uses for our salvation. God will see you through—just don't quit.

Someone is watching you in the storm. You have the opportunity to be to someone in your life what Paul was to his shipmates—a source of comfort, encouragement, faith, and good cheer. You can be light and salt to a hurting world. You have many people—family, relatives, friends, coworkers, neighbors, and lost people—that you probably don't even realize are watching you. Stand up and say, "Everything is going to be all right. I believe God." Be a testimony to God's grace and goodness. You may save others from the storm.

I read a touching story about a family who was expecting their second child. When they found out about the pregnancy, they began working to prepare their three-year-old son Michael for the arrival. They found out they would have a girl, and Michael would sing to his sister in Mommy's tummy. He built a bond of love with her even before she was born. The pregnancy progressed normally, but when it was time to deliver the baby there were complications. After a long and difficult labor, the baby was born, but she was in very serious condition.

The baby was transferred to the neonatal intensive care unit at St. Mary's Hospital in Knoxville, Tennessee. Days passed, and the little girl got worse. The pediatrician told them that there was not much hope. The parents with broken hearts purchased a plot at a cemetery where their daughter would be buried. They had prepared a nursery in their home for the new arrival; now they were planning a funeral.

Michael kept begging his parents to let him see his sister. "I want to sing to her," he said. Two weeks passed, and Michael continued to ask to see her. Of course, children aren't allowed into intensive care, so he could not. Finally his mother decided to take him in anyhow. If he didn't see his sister then, he would never have the chance to see her alive. She put him into a scrub suit—it was way too big to fit—and walked into the unit. The nurse saw him and said, "Get that kid out of here. No children are allowed." The mother glared at the nurse and said, "He's not leaving until he sings to his sister."

She took Michael to the incubator where his sister was losing her fight for life. Michael began to sing "You Are My Sunshine." Instantly the baby girl seemed to respond. Her pulse became steady. Her breathing eased and became normal. His mother told him to keep singing. Everyone in the room was weeping and watching in disbelief. The next day the girl was well enough to go home. The version I read of this story was called "The Miracle of a Brother's Song." I don't know that every detail of this story is correct—often stories like this get changed or exaggerated as they are passed around and retold—but I do know this: When you trust God and give thanks in your storms, He works miracles! And your proper response has a powerful impact on those around you.

FIVE

The Spirit of Fear

I thank God, whom I serve from my forefathers with pure conscience, that without ceasing I have remembrance of thee in my prayers night and day; Greatly desiring to see thee, being mindful of thy tears, that I may be filled with joy; When I call to remembrance the unfeigned faith that is in thee, which dwelt first in thy grandmother Lois, and thy mother Eunice; and I am persuaded that in thee also. Wherefore I put thee in remembrance that thou stir up the gift of God, which is in thee by the putting on of my hands. For God hath not given us the spirit of fear; but of power, and of love, and of a sound mind.—2 TIMOTHY 1:3–7

Once someone asked me for help and counseling. The person he was working with had hit a roadblock. The counselor thought the person was resisting what he had to say, and the person he was trying to help thought the counselor simply didn't understand the situation. After I got a few more details on the situation, I said, "It sounds like a misunderstanding of the difference between fear and rebellion."

Many times what we see as rebellious behavior is actually the result of fear. Attempting to overcome the perceived rebellion doesn't address the real problem and won't lead to a successful resolution. The devil doesn't care whether he dares you into sin (rebellion) or scares you into sin (fear). Though I believe most sin is motivated by fear rather than rebellion, most of our preaching and teaching focuses on rebellion rather than fear. Let's look at what the Bible has to say about fear and examine ways we can overcome it.

THE REVELATION OF FEAR

In this passage from Paul to his young protégé Timothy, we see that fear is a spirit. Note that the Bible does not say that being afraid is a sin. My father told me, "The man who says he is not afraid of anything is either a liar or a fool." The psalmist wrote, *"What time I am afraid, I will trust in thee"* (Psalm 56:3). What the Bible tells us is that a life controlled by an attitude of fear does not come from God.

If a spirit of fear doesn't come from God, from whence does it come? Only two spiritual forces are in the world: God and the devil. If fear doesn't come from God, there is only one other possible source. Not only does God not give us a spirit of fear, He tells us to overcome fear. More than two hundred times in Scripture we find commands like, "fear not" and "be not afraid."

Your nervousness, hesitancy, and fear of what people are going to think keep you from doing service for the Lord and are not from God. We allow fear to stop us from agreeing to teach a Sunday school class, to work on a bus route, to go soulwinning, to tithe. That pleases the devil greatly because he wins. It's true that some people who are greedy and self-centered want to go their own way and do their own thing. We tend to focus on them rather than those who do not do right because of fear.

We have wicked hearts and are prone to rebellion against God. Yet over and over I've seen good people who generally want to do right fail because of fear. While few Christians don't care if the whole world dies and goes to Hell, most do care. But why don't they go soulwinning? In large measure it is because of a spirit of fear. What if they are rude to me? What if they have a mean dog? What if they ask a question I can't answer? What if I get embarrassed and say something wrong? That is the spirit of fear in action.

People are not born with an innate appetite for drugs, alcohol, or tobacco. I've talked to people about their reaction the first time they tried one of those. They didn't like it. It is possible to develop a taste for such things—and they can become powerful addictions—but it doesn't start out that way. Statistics tell us that most people who experiment with those things do so at a very young age—usually 12 or 13. Why? Because their friends encourage them through peer pressure. Fear of not fitting in or being mocked leads them to wrong behavior.

I've seen pure, young Christian ladies start dating guys who have no desire for Christ. I want to say, "Why? What do you see in him? What is the dynamic?" I've also had some of those young ladies come to me in tears and confess that they have lost their purity. Now some might say, "I have done right and God hasn't blessed me, so I'm just going to go out and live my life the way I want." That's rare. More often they do wrong because of fear and insecurity.

Statistics tell us that most people who claim to be Christians don't tithe. Sure, probably a few feel, "I worked for that money, and it's mine, so I don't care what the Bible says; I'm going to keep it." But most people know they should tithe. They feel badly about not tithing, and it burdens them that they don't put God's money in the offering plate when it goes by. They wish they could, but they are afraid if they do they won't be able to pay their bills. It is usually not rebellion that motivates us to disobey God; it's fear.

THE RIGHT FEAR

Not all fear is bad. Fear that is right, proper, and even required is the fear of the Lord. Proverbs 9:10 says, *"The fear of the LORD is the beginning of wisdom…."* Now that seems to be a contradiction. If God doesn't give us the spirit of fear, how can we rightly fear Him? To understand that, we first have to understand what it means to fear God. I have heard a lot of people say that it means respect or reverence for God. That sounds good, but if you look up the word fear, it means fear.

Let me illustrate it this way. I love my dad. I still love to talk to him on the phone. I still get advice from him. When I was a kid, I loved to go places with him—hunting, fishing, preaching. I couldn't wait for him to get home—except on those occasions when I had been misbehaving. My mother would say, "Just wait till your father gets home." I did not greet him in the driveway on those days. Why? Because, though I loved my father, I had not been obedient. We should have a terror of displeasing God.

Proverbs 29:25 says, *"The fear of man bringeth a snare: but whoso putteth his trust in the LORD shall be safe."* Proverbs 14:26 says, *"In the fear of the LORD is strong confidence: and his children shall have a place of refuge."* Look at the contrast: if you fear man, you will be held captive; if you fear God, you will be confident. When we fear God, we have a fear of the right thing.

Jesus said, *"And fear not them which kill the body, but are not able to kill the soul: but rather fear him which is able to destroy both soul and body in hell"* (Matthew 10:28). Who destroys people in Hell? It's not Satan; it is a holy God exercising justice on those who reject salvation in Jesus Christ. The only thing God's children should fear is Him.

THE REASONS FOR FEAR

The word Paul uses when he talks of the spirit of fear occurs nowhere else in the New Testament. In classical Greek it refers to cowardice. It is actually a compound word, made up of the words for timid and faithless. Lack of faith and the presence of fear are connected. Fearful people are faithless people. Faithful people fear less. Sometimes we think of faith as absolute certainty, a tremendous confidence and complete assurance that everything will work out just fine.

The three Hebrew children when threatened with the burning fiery furnace said, "...*our God whom we serve is able to deliver us...But if not...we will not serve thy gods...*" (Daniel 3:17–18). Doubt was mixed in with their bold pronouncement of faith in God. They had some hesitation in their hearts, but they still did right. Dr. John Rice said that if you put a dot on one side of the paper and call it total unbelief and a dot on the other side and call it absolute certainty, then anything in between those dots is faith. In this regard my definition of faith is trusting God 1% more than you trust your doubts.

At times when God has led me to give something financially, even after all these years and years of giving and seeing God bless, it makes me stop and think, "I don't know if I can do that." Sometimes I am still fearful, but when I write the check and put it in the offering plate, that's faith. If I were to keep the money, I would be living in bondage to the spirit of fear. It is not the absence of doubt that demonstrates faith; it is acting in obedience to God's Word.

I'm always intrigued when I read the story of Gideon. He gathered an army of 32,000 soldiers. That meant they were still outnumbered more than four to one, but God said, "You have too many people. If you win the victory, I won't get all of the glory." So God told Gideon to send home all those who were afraid. Twenty-two thousand of the men went home. The Bible doesn't tell us how it happened, but I suspect that probably one person said to his friend, "I think we may as well go home." Then when another man saw them leaving, he decided to leave too. Pretty soon they were leaving by the hundreds. Fear is contagious.

We see the same thing happen in the story of the twelve spies Moses sent into the land of Canaan. Ten of them returned and told the people about the giants in the land and the great walled cities, and they discouraged the people. Only Joshua and Caleb said that God would deliver the people into their hand. Those ten spies discouraged the entire nation of Israel, and they refused to obey God. As a result of that faithlessness, they wandered in the wilderness for forty years until all of the adults were dead. They weren't rebelling against God so much as they were fearful and thus disobedient.

Understand this: though our sin is often motivated by fear rather than rebellion, it is still sin. It is just as sinful to drink the booze because you're scared of what your coworkers will say about you as it is to drink because you want to get drunk. It's just as sinful to hold back the tithe because you're afraid you won't be able to pay your bills as it is to think it's your money and you can do what you want with it. It is not sinful to be afraid, but it is sinful to let a spirit of fear make your decision.

THE RESULTS OF FEAR

What happens when we allow fear to rule our lives? First, there is a *separation*. We see this in the story of Adam and Eve. They lived in perfect harmony and fellowship with God. Then sin entered the picture when Adam ate the fruit of the tree of the knowledge of good and evil. When it was time for God to come to talk with them, Adam and Eve hid. Genesis 3:9–10 says, *"And the LORD God called unto Adam, and said unto him, Where art thou? And he said, I heard thy voice in the garden, and I was afraid, because I was naked; and I hid myself."* Adam had heard God's voice every day of his life. It was a sweet and welcome sound before; now it made him afraid. Fear separated Adam from God.

Fear also brings a *snare*. Earlier we saw this truth in Proverbs 29:25 which says, *"The fear of man bringeth a snare."* Fear entraps and controls us. We had a teacher in our school many years ago who instructed his students not to tell their parents if he did something in the classroom he thought the parents might not like. The students would then use that against him to get more leeway from him by threatening to tell their parents. Fear entangled him and kept him from doing right. By the way, he doesn't teach for us anymore.

Fear can become a *self-fulfilling prophecy*. Job said, *"The thing which I greatly feared is come upon me, and that which I was afraid of is come unto me. I was not in safety, neither had I rest, neither was I quiet; yet trouble came"* (Job 3:25–26). If you are always looking for some terrible event to occur, you may inadvertently behave in ways to make it occur. I have counseled with hurt people who said, "Every person I ever loved has turned their back on me and left." I don't think those people intentionally try to make that happen, but I've seen them subconsciously behave in such a way that they drive people away from them.

Fear can also make us *sin*. When God came and told Abraham that Sarah would have a son, she was listening in the tent, and she laughed. She was nearly ninety years old, and Abraham was nearly one hundred. What God was saying just didn't make sense. But when God asked her about it, she lied. Why? Because she was afraid. Fear keeps people from doing right. Fear leads people to give in to temptation and do wrong. Fear is a dangerous spirit; so what can we do about it?

THE RESOURCES FOR OVERCOMING FEAR

The Scripture tells us that God has given us three specific resources to help us defeat the spirit of fear. *There is the resource of power.* The Greek word for power is *dunamis*, from which we get the word *dynamite*. We do not operate in our own power but in God's power. Just before He returned to Heaven, Jesus told the disciples, "*All power is given unto me in heaven and in earth. Go ye therefore, and teach all nations, baptizing them in the name of the Father, and of the Son, and of the Holy Ghost*" (Matthew 28:18–19).

When we try to operate in our power, we may fall prey to fear. I can't preach the Gospel, lead people to Christ, and pastor the First Baptist Church of Bridgeport in my strength. If I rely on that, I am likely to be ruled by fear. How do you respond to your weaknesses? Paul was bothered by his weaknesses until he learned what they were meant to accomplish. He said, "*…Most* *gladly therefore will I rather glory in my infirmities, that the power of Christ may rest upon me"* (2 Corinthians 12:9).

God isn't looking for strong people who can help Him out. God is looking for people who are fully aware of their weaknesses and willing to place themselves in His hand so that for what they accomplish in His power He gets the glory. God delights in using unlikely people in His work. Paul said, *"For ye see your calling, brethren, how that not many wise men after the flesh, not many mighty, not many noble, are called: But God hath chosen the foolish things of the world to confound the wise; and God hath chosen the weak things of the world to confound the things which are mighty; And base things of the world, and things which are despised, hath God chosen, yea, and things which are not, to bring to nought things that are: That no flesh should glory in his presence"* (1 Corinthians 1:26–29).

I've often had people come up to me and say, "You were preaching on such and such, and when you said that, God really used it to help me with this or that." Many times I have thought to myself, "I don't remember saying that." In fact, sometimes I've been quite sure I never said that. I do think they heard it, but I don't think I said it. I believe when we get to Heaven we will be amazed at the impact of the little things we did in obedience to God and in reliance on the power of His Spirit. When you are faced with fear, when you think you are weak and cannot do what needs to be done, you're right. In those moments God's power is available to you to overcome your fear and do what He has called you to do.

There is the resource of love. First John 4:18 says, *"There is no fear in love; but perfect love casteth out fear: because fear hath torment. He that feareth is not made perfect in love."* People will do things for love that they would otherwise be afraid to do. Many of the things we are called to do are uncomfortable for us, but we do them because of our love for Jesus Christ. Paul said it this way: *"For the love of Christ constraineth us"* (2 Corinthians 5:14).

When you are struggling with obedience in some area, especially if fear is keeping you from doing right, picture Jesus asking you to do it as a favor. How do you think you would respond if you were looking into His eyes and seeing His nail-scarred hands? I don't think it would be easy for any of us to say no to Jesus directly. He died for us. He saved us. He lives and makes intercession for us. His love compels our response.

Not long ago I was flying home from preaching on the West Coast. The last plane was a small one, just two seats on each side. I was in the aisle seat on the emergency exit row. The man with the window seat came in, and I moved to let him by. As he was getting into his seat he dropped his glasses. As I picked them up and handed them to him, he thanked me. I pulled out a tract from our church and asked, "Can I give you something I wrote?" He looked at it, saw what it was and said, "Nah." He wouldn't speak to me the rest of the flight. I could allow that to make me afraid to pass out tracts on my next trip, but the love God has put in my heart for lost people compels me to keep trying. That love casts out my fear of rejection.

Do not expect the world to love you—rely on God's love instead. Jesus said, *"If the world hate you, ye know that it hated me before it hated you. If ye were of the world, the world would love his own: but because ye are not of the world, but I have chosen you out of the world, therefore the world hateth you. Remember the word that I said unto you, The servant is not greater than his lord. If they have persecuted me, they will also persecute you; if they have kept my saying, they will keep yours also"* (John 15:18–20).

There is the resource of a sound mind. The phrase *sound mind* comes from a root word that means "a disciplined or developed mind." When I go to the YMCA, I don't like any of it. I don't like lifting weights. I don't enjoy the Nordic Track ski machine. I don't appreciate working out. I started going there to strengthen my muscles to give me relief from back pain I was having. On the way there I try to think of some reason to do something else instead. I always want to stop instead of finishing the different parts of my workout. I never do, but I always want to. Why do I do it anyway? Because I know it is good for me. I exercise because it allows me to serve God actively as long as I can.

I discipline my body so I can do what God has for me to do. We need to do the same with our minds. Not every thought you have is acceptable to God. Your thoughts are only as valuable as they are consistent with the Scriptures. So many people are impressed with what they think, but they have no Bible basis for their opinions. We are supposed to bring every thought we have into captivity and force it to obey Christ (2 Corinthians 10:5). It is harder to discipline your mind than it is to discipline your body, but it's way more important.

What does it mean to discipline our minds regarding fear? When a thought comes like, "Oh, no! What am I going to do?"

replace it with, "What does God want me to do or learn in this situation?" Instead of, "How will I buy groceries and pay the bills if I tithe?" ask, "How can I be blessed if I disobey God?" Rather than thinking, "If I witness to him he'll laugh at me or get mad," think, "God loves him, and wants me to share the Gospel with him." You can control your thoughts; you must control your thoughts. Constantly correct your wrong thinking.

Wayne van Gelderen, Sr. was the speaker for my college baccaluareate service. He said, "As you go out into the world, you will be constantly bombarded with wrong ideas. They come from everywhere. The only way to keep your mind right is to immediately correct every wrong idea." You won't have a sound mind unless you work at it—not just once or twice, but on a continual basis. It's even more important to correct the wrong thoughts you have internally than the wrong ideas you see and hear.

Allow the Word of God to fill and control your mind. Meditate on the Scriptures you have memorized. Use the Bible as the standard against which you measure every thought and every idea. If they don't agree, change your thinking rather than trying to change the Bible to agree with you. This process will free you from fear. There is no reason to be afraid if your thoughts are controlled by the promises of God.

THE REMEDY FOR FEAR

Choose the right fear. You can choose to fear God, or you can choose to fear man. Proverbs 1:29 tells of people who *"hated knowledge, and did not choose the fear of the* LORD." No one fears God by accident; we come to the fear of the Lord by controlling our thinking and bringing it in line with the Word. To review, you are responsible for what you think, and you can control it so that you choose the right fear.

Walk by faith. You do what you do because of who you believe most. All of us have competing voices vying for control. All of us are tempted to make our own decisions and employ human wisdom. Who knows better, you or God? It doesn't take long to answer that question. You don't have to study and weigh the evidence; God knows better. Yet time and again we choose to walk by what we see and what makes sense to us rather than by what He says in His Word. Faith is listening to God more than you listen to your doubts and fears.

Review God's promises. Learn these verses and use them. (Where did we get the idea that Bible memory is only for children?) Let me share just a handful of God's promises with you.

- Psalm 34:7 promises us protection.
- Psalm 34:9 promises us provision.
- Psalm 85:9 promises us pardon.
- Psalm 103:13 promises us pity.
- Proverbs 14:26 promises us power.

Wait for God to work. Do NOT take matters into your own hands. Many times we miss the blessing because we don't wait quite long enough to receive. When Israel was fleeing from Egypt, they came to the Red Sea. Mountains surrounded both sides of them, and Pharaoh and his army were coming from behind them. Moses told them to *"stand still, and see the salvation of the Lord"* (Exodus 14:13). They waited until God parted the Red Sea, and then they walked across on dry ground.

Keep on believing. Luke 8 tells us the story of Jairus who came to Jesus because his twelve-year-old daughter was dying. While they were on the way to his house, Jesus was touched by the woman who had the issue of blood, and He stopped to talk to her. During the delay, someone came and told Jairus that it was too late—that his daughter was dead. Jesus said to him, *"Fear not, believe only"* (Luke 8:50). Jairus had enough faith to ask Jesus to heal his sick daughter, but it hadn't occurred to him that Jesus could raise his daughter from the dead.

We have a mental framework of how things could work out. We picture a check coming in the mail or getting a raise at work (or getting a job), but God often works beyond our imagination. Do not allow your faith to be limited by what you can figure out. You don't have to construct the means of your deliverance. Whatever else you do, keep believing. When you're afraid, believe. When you're in need, believe. When you don't see the way out, believe. You can trust Him in every circumstance.

SIX

The Bitter Widow

Now it came to pass in the days when the judges ruled, that there was a famine in the land. And a certain man of Bethlehemjudah went to sojourn in the country of Moab, he, and his wife, and his two sons. And the name of the man was Elimelech, and the name of his wife Naomi, and the name of his two sons Mahlon and Chilion, Ephrathites of Bethlehemjudah. And they came into the country of Moab, and continued there. And Elimelech Naomi's husband died; and she was left, and her two sons. And they took them wives of the women of Moab; the name of the one was Orpah, and the name of the other Ruth: and they dwelled there about ten years. And Mahlon and Chilion died also both of them; and the woman was left of her two sons and her husband. Then she arose with her daughters in law, that she might return from the country of Moab: for she had heard in the country of Moab how that the LORD *had visited his people in giving them bread. Wherefore she went forth out of the place where she was, and her two daughters in law with her; and they went on the way to return unto the land of Judah. And Naomi said unto her two daughters in law, Go, return each to her mother's house: the LORD deal kindly with you, as ye have dealt with the dead, and with me. The LORD grant you that ye may find rest, each of you in the house of her husband. Then she kissed them; and they lifted up their voice, and wept.*—RUTH 1:1–9

The story of Naomi and Ruth begins with a lack of faith. Because of the famine, Elimelech took his family and moved away from the land God promised to the Jews to live among the heathen Moabites. Because of that decision, both of his sons married women from that land. As it always does, human wisdom failed, and Elimelech and his sons died. That left Naomi alone in a strange land without her husband or children, and as we see in these verses, she decided to return to Bethlehem.

As you read the account of Naomi's life, it's hard to understand how she commanded such loyalty from Ruth. The only conclusion you can reach (from the part of the story we're told in Scripture) is that it was because of Ruth's character rather than Naomi's conduct that Ruth returned to Israel to care for her widowed mother-in-law. Everything we see about Naomi reeks of bitterness. She had lost her confidence in God, and she appeared to have no hope for the future.

THE CONDITION

As this story opens, we see a family with a great heritage. Naomi lived in Bethlehem. In light of the famine that led them to move away, it's a bit ironic that Bethlehem means "house of bread." It was a place where God provided for, sustained, and supplied the needs of His people. It was a place where God encouraged His people and a place God had promised to His people.

Naomi was married to a man named Elimelech. In Bible times, names had great meaning, and Elimelech means "God is my king." Naomi and Elimelech were of the tribe of Judah, the tribe from which the Messiah would come. The Scripture refers to them as Ephrathites, a name that means "fruitful." These people were connected to God's plan in God's place. But circumstances didn't stay good. During the time of the judges, a famine came into the land, putting much stress on Naomi and her family.

It was a time of hunger. Hard times are not new. The biggest difference between the hard times we're having today and the hard times of the past is that today we aren't worried about starving to death. Many people have lost their jobs and their homes. Many are worried about their retirement accounts and how they will pay for their kids' college, but we're not seeing people die for lack of food.

Naomi and Elimelech made the decision to "sojourn" in the land of Moab. The Hebrew word translated *sojourn* means "to turn aside from the road"; it has the idea of being a guest.

They were only planning to stay for a little while, until the famine ended and things got better.

The Atlanta airport has a restaurant called the "Sojourners Cafe." Those who eat there are on their way to somewhere else. It's not a destination restaurant; it's a place to stop for a little while.

Their plan changed. They went there as guests, but after a while they became residents. Ten years later, they were still in Moab. Both of their sons married girls from Moab. Few things in life are more dangerous than deciding to turn aside from the road of God's will temporarily. From time to time we've had young people from our church go off to a Christian college and run into financial difficulty. They will say something like, "I'm going to drop out for one semester and work. Then when I get some money saved up, I'll go back." In almost every case they never go back.

The names of Naomi's sons shed light on the condition of her heart. Mahlon means "sick" or "puny" and Chilion means "pining," as in someone who has consumption or a wasting disease. You think you were teased on the playground when you were little? Try going to school with the name Puny or Pining! I have a little experience with that kind of thing. When my parents found out they were expecting, my mother wanted to name me after my father, but he thought it would be hard on me to be called Junior. He was studying French, and he thought Rene, which means "new birth," would be a good name. My mother's maiden name was Bock, and there weren't any boys in her family, so she thought it would be good to carry on the family name in that way. Now, I tell people R. B. stands for real butter, but I went through school with the name Rene Bock Ouellette. I think Junior might have been easier to deal with!

These names were given to the boys *before* the family went to Moab. From the very beginning of their lives, Naomi was somewhat negative toward her two boys. She had an attitude problem, not because of the famine and the hard times, but before any of this even started. Negative people have a hard time appreciating the blessings of God.

THE CONSEQUENCES

We don't know if Elimelech, Mahlon, and Chilion would have died had they stayed in Bethlehem. Their situation was bad, but their solution made things worse. Both sons ended up marrying Moabites. The Israelites had been specifically commanded not to marry pagan women. *"Neither shalt thou make marriages with them; thy daughter thou shalt not give unto his son, nor his daughter shalt thou take unto thy son. For they will turn away thy son from following me, that they may serve other gods: so will the anger of the* Lord *be kindled against you, and destroy thee suddenly"* (Deuteronomy 7:3–4).

If I could ask Naomi a question, it would probably be: "What did you expect?" If you move away from God's people to live among the pagans, who are they going to marry? You need to be careful about the environment in which you rear your children. Be careful about where they work, where they go to school, who they spend time with, and what they do. If their lives are filled with influences that are contrary to the Word of God, don't be surprised if they get off track.

Eventually Naomi made a discovery. She decided to go back to Bethlehem because she heard the news that God had provided bread for His people in the Promised Land. God always sustains those people who stay in His will. Provision doesn't come from a place; it comes from a Person. Your hope is in the Lord. I'm not saying that you should never move to a different location, but you certainly should never leave the will of God. The people who stayed in Bethlehem received the provision of bread that God provided.

Never move just because you're hungry for something else. Never move just because the economy is better somewhere else. Never move because you're scared. Dr. Bill Rice had a picture that hung in his office for many years of two horses standing on opposite sides of a fence. Each of them was reaching his head over the fence to eat the grass on the other side! Too often that's the way we are. We think the grass is greener somewhere else, but it's not. Only make a move when God is leading you to make a move. Finally, Naomi went back to where she should have stayed in the first place. But I want you to notice that even though she was headed in the right direction, she still had a heart problem—a bad attitude that she was taking back to Bethlehem with her.

THE COMPLAINT

Naomi said, "...*the hand of the LORD is gone out against me.... the Almighty hath dealt very bitterly with me*" (Ruth 1:13, 20). Isn't it amazing how we blame God for our mistakes and missteps? It wasn't God's fault that Naomi left where she should have stayed. It wasn't God's fault that she refused to trust Him. It wasn't God's fault that she walked by sight rather than by faith. It was Naomi's fault, yet she blamed God and was bitter about the consequences of her own decisions and actions. If you follow your own plan and your own desires, don't be surprised if you don't like the results.

Understand this truth: whenever you blame God, you're wrong. He never makes mistakes. He is never unjust. You may not understand Him; you may not see His plan, but He always does right. If you read the book of Job, you'll see that over and over Job says that he wishes he could give God a piece of his mind. When God showed up, Job said, *"I abhor myself, and repent in dust and ashes"* (Job 42:6). When you realize who and what God is, you won't blame Him for anything.

Of all the statements Naomi made, perhaps this is the most revealing. She said, *"I went out full, and the LORD hath brought me home again empty"* (Ruth 1:21). When things get stressful, whether financially, emotionally or physically, we often think "It can't get worse than this." Yes, it can. Many times I've heard people look back and say something like, "I didn't know how good I had it." Naomi left where she should have been because she thought they were hungry; now she knew what true emptiness really was as she returned home without her husband and her sons. Naomi told the people of Bethlehem to call her Mara, which means "bitter."

We see in this story that Naomi took no responsibility for all the bad things that happened. She blamed it all on God, falsely accusing Him of being unfair in His dealings with her. "Why would God do this to me?" When people come to me for counsel who are struggling with their finances, my first question is always, "Are you tithing?" Would you like to take a guess at how many of those people have said, "Yes"? (It's a pretty small number!) Yet we get mad at God because things aren't going the way we think they should.

It's part of human nature that we don't appreciate God's protection. In Malachi 3:11 God says, *"And I will rebuke the devourer for your sakes."* Yet I almost never hear anyone say, "I didn't have a flat tire this week." "I'm rejoicing because my roof didn't leak." "God is so good because my lawnmower kept running." Sometimes God blesses us in ways that are imperceptible—we don't see them unless we're looking for them. Naomi blamed God for everything that was wrong in her life, but gave Him no thanks or credit for the things that went right.

Naomi took no responsibility for her attitude. She was bitter and complaining—and as we saw she had attitude problems even before the family left Bethlehem. Picture Paul and Silas in the jail at Philippi behaving as Naomi did instead of rejoicing. If they had been griping and complaining, saying, "The Lord has dealt bitterly with us; the Lord has made us empty," do you think the jailer would have wanted to know how to get saved? Your circumstances should not dictate your attitude. You can rejoice no matter what is going on; in fact, you are supposed to. From his prison cell in Rome Paul wrote, *"Rejoice in the Lord alway: and again I say, Rejoice"* (Philippians 4:4).

Naomi took no responsibility for her actions. She and her husband did not have to leave Bethlehem and look for greener pastures in a heathen nation. She did not have to give her sons negative names. Yet she never once expressed any repentance or regret; she just complained. I read about a ruler in ancient times who paid a visit to a prison. As he went from man to man, each one proclaimed his innocence. Finally, he came to one man who admitted he deserved to be where he was. "Release this criminal at once," the ruler commanded. "It is not right for all these innocent men to be forced to remain in his company." If your circumstances are partly the result of what you have done (or not done), be willing to confess it and repent.

Naomi expressed no gratitude for Ruth's affection. Naomi told both of her daughters-in-law to stay in Moab when she decided to return to Bethlehem. Orpah agreed, but Ruth made the beautiful declaration that today we often hear at weddings. *"And Ruth said, Intreat me not to leave thee, or to return from following after thee: for whither thou goest, I will go; and where thou lodgest, I will lodge: thy people shall be my people, and thy God my God: Where thou diest, will I die, and there will I be buried: the* LORD *do so to me, and more also, if ought but death part thee and me"* (Ruth 1:16–17). Yet in the face of that incredible display of love, loyalty, and devotion, Naomi said, "I came home empty." She did not appreciate the great gifts she had been given.

THE CONCLUSIONS

Never leave the place of blessing unless God tells you to. I've never been in the military, but people who have been have told me that you always carry out the last order you had until you get a new order. You don't need peace to stay; you need peace to leave. Sometimes God takes people away from the place of blessing. He took Philip away from a great revival to go to the wilderness and witness to just one man. He took Joseph away from his family and home so he would make preparations in Egypt to save them from the famine. God does lead people to move at times, but you should never make a move simply because of hard times.

You usually have more than you think you do. Why did Naomi and Elimelech leave Bethlehem? Because of the famine. Yet when Naomi came back, she had learned enough to realize that when she went out, she was full. We tend to measure our blessings by the number and size of our belongings; God measures them according to a different standard—His purpose for our lives. Looking back, we often see that things were not as bad as we thought they were at the time and that it was actually during the troubled times that we saw God's greatest work.

No matter how bad it seems in the will of God, it is worse out of the will of God. Jonah thought the worst thing in the world would be for him to go to Nineveh and preach so that the people would repent. He found out that things could get worse. It amazes me that it took three days in the belly of the great fish before Jonah started praying. He was stubborn; I think he may have been one of the first Baptist preachers. I am not saying that we never struggle in the will of God. Both the Bible and our own experience prove that we do. I am saying that if you run from God's place, your situation will not improve.

Your material decisions will have a major impact on the spiritual future of your children. Naomi went to Moab to find a better life, not to find heathen wives for her sons, yet that is what happened. I will never forget a time as a teenager when my father urgently needed to sell a house. Finally, a man came along and agreed to buy the house if my father would overstate the sales price so he could get a larger loan from the mortgage company. My father declined. He would have been much better off in the short term to have taken the money, but he set a standard for honesty and integrity before my young eyes that has paid dividends for decades in my life.

God always takes care of His children who stay in His place. God does not promise to give you all you want, but He does promise to give you all you need. He may use unusual means, like the ravens He sent to feed Elijah during the famine. He may take you through storms and shipwrecks, as He did with Paul on his journey to Rome. But He will always provide. David said, *"I have been young, and now am old: yet have I not seen the righteous forsaken, nor his seed begging bread"* (Psalm 37:25). God will keep all of His promises.

There are blessings even in Moab. Even when we make mistakes, God's mercy is so great that He does good things, sometimes even in spite of ourselves. The people of Israel did not obey the command of God to keep the Sabbath for 490 years. So for 70 years they were held captive in Babylon. Yet even during that time, God blessed them and multiplied them and gave them peace (Jeremiah 29:5–7). Though she was in the wrong place living in Moab, God still gave Naomi the great blessing of a loyal friend in Ruth.

The most impressive love is that which is directed at the unlovely. If Naomi had been sweet and kind, it would be easy to understand why Ruth loved her so much. Yet despite Naomi's bitterness and lack of appreciation, Ruth loved her. Sometimes people who are in trouble are hard to love, yet it is at those times that they need love the most. God loved us when we were unlovely. We need to extend that same love and grace to others. Troubled times often present you with an opportunity to show God's love to people as never before.

We must not blame God when we make incorrect choices. I've heard people say, "I know what I'm going through is because of my sin, but…." I always stop them there. If there's a "but," you haven't learned the lesson yet. God is not to blame for your wrong choices, nor for the consequences that may follow from them.

A father called me for help who had been separated from his children because of sin. He straightened out his life and thought he would get his children back; when he didn't, he returned to his sin. I told him, "You do right, not because it will get your children back, but because it is right."

Though Naomi shows us largely negative lessons, they are important ones for us to remember during troubled times. And one lesson is perhaps more vital than any other—as long as you're still alive, you can still return to God. You may not regain everything you lost; however, you may gain new blessings as never before. Naomi saw Ruth marry a great man named Boaz and got to hold her grandson, who in turn would have a grandson named David. If you are still here, God still has things for you to do, no matter how troubled your life may be. Start your return journey to Bethlehem today. Return to the place of blessing and leave your bitterness behind.

SEVEN

The Burdened Widow

Now there cried a certain woman of the wives of the sons of the prophets unto Elisha, saying, Thy servant my husband is dead; and thou knowest that thy servant did fear the LORD: and the creditor is come to take unto him my two sons to be bondmen. And Elisha said unto her, What shall I do for thee? tell me, what hast thou in the house? And she said, Thine handmaid hath not any thing in the house, save a pot of oil. Then he said, Go, borrow thee vessels abroad of all thy neighbours, even empty vessels; borrow not a few. And when thou art come in, thou shalt shut the door upon thee and upon thy sons, and shalt pour out into all those vessels, and thou shalt set aside that which is full. So she went from him, and shut the door upon her and upon her sons, who brought the vessels to her; and she poured out. And it came to pass, when the vessels were full, that she said unto her son, Bring me yet a vessel. And

he said unto her, There is not a vessel more. And the oil stayed.
Then she came and told the man of God. And he said, Go, sell the
oil, and pay thy debt, and live thou and thy children of the rest.
—2 KINGS 4:1–7

In Bible days perhaps one of the most vulnerable members of society was a widow. Life insurance did not exist in those days, and there were very few ways for a woman without a husband to make a living. It was particularly hard for those widows who had children for whom to provide. Moses instructed the children of Israel to leave the corners of their fields alone when they gleaned during the harvest. Those who were poor, including the widows, could then come and gather food for themselves and their families.

The widow in this story was in even worse condition than normal, for her husband had been in debt when he died. She came to Elisha for help because the creditor was preparing to take her two sons as payment for the debt. We are long past the days of debtor's prison or people being put in bondage for their unpaid loans. Her reality was grim. The one thing she knew was that God's prophet offered help and hope when no one else did.

THE WIDOW'S APPEAL

This widow's husband was a student in the school of the prophets under Elisha. The sons of the prophets were not the children of prophets but rather those who were studying for a life of ministry and service to God under the prophet. The widow came and reminded Elisha of that relationship and asked him for help. She based her appeal on her deceased husband's faith in God and his fear of the Lord. This was a man who believed right and behaved right, but he had made some unwise financial decisions. Her appeal was also based on her burden. Having already lost her husband, she was now facing the loss of her two sons.

I'm fascinated by Elisha's response to the widow. Remember that Elisha was a man of means. When Elijah visited Elisha to call him to the ministry, Elisha was plowing with twelve yoke of oxen. For a family to have one ox would have been good, but to have twenty-four would indicate a great deal of wealth. Imagine you are a person of some means and a widow comes to you and asks for help. What would you say? I think for most of us the first thing we would say is, "How much money do you need?" That's not what Elisha did.

If the need were great and our hearts were stirred but we didn't have the means to meet it, perhaps we would try to get others to help meet it. Our church supported a good and godly missionary, and then I found out that his mission board wasn't treating him right. I told him, "If you feel that God is leading you to leave that mission board, I will personally take responsibility for calling pastors to replace any support you lose." That's not what Elisha did either.

I don't think Elisha lacked compassion, but you might think so from his response. He asked, "What shall I do for thee?" Basically, he asked her what she wanted him to do about it. Then Elisha asked her about her possessions. Now this seems like a strange question. She had already told them about their problem with debt. Clearly they didn't have much in the way of resources. We tend to focus on what we don't have; God wants us to focus on what we do have. What do you have in your house today?

This is a pattern we see often repeated in Scripture. God used the shepherd's staff that Moses had in his hand as an instrument of power to deliver Israel from bondage in Egypt. God used the sling that David had in his hand to slay Goliath. God used the lunch of one little boy to feed more than five thousand with plenty left over. God is able to use whatever you have, no matter how small it is, to accomplish His purposes. Rather than wishing you had greater resources, put those you do have to work. You will be amazed to see what God does with what you give to Him.

ELISHA'S ANSWER

Elisha had the power of God on his life in an unusual way. When Elijah was preparing to be taken to Heaven, he offered to do something for Elisha, and Elisha asked for a double portion of the spirit of Elijah (2 Kings 2:9). He could have performed a great miracle in front of the students at the school of the prophets. He could have publicly done something to meet this widow's great need. Instead he gave her a set of instructions that required her to act in faith before seeing any results. We don't know for sure, but I think Elisha involved the two boys in the process so that they would see firsthand the power of God and their faith would be strengthened.

Elisha's response required the widow to take action—the plan he presented to her demanded her effort. The results we get from God often depend on our actions. Sometimes in difficult circumstances we expect a divine rescue without any work on our part. That may happen, but usually God expects us to do what we can for ourselves before He works on our behalf.

We see this same type of process used when Elisha was old and nearing death. He called King Joash to come see him. The story is found in 2 Kings 13. Elisha had the king shoot an arrow out the window toward Syria with his hands on the king's hands; it was what the old prophet called the "arrow of the LORD's deliverance." Then Elisha told the king to strike the rest of the arrows on the ground. Joash did it only three times. I wonder if he felt that what he was being asked to do was silly. Regardless, Elisha was angry. He told Joash that if he had struck the arrows five or six times God would have given him complete victory over Syria; instead now he would have only three victories.

The faith you demonstrate in doing what you are given to do may well determine how much blessing you receive from God. So Elisha instructed the widow to borrow vessels from her neighbors—"borrow not a few."

Seeing this miracle and being part of it must have had a powerful impact on the widow's sons. Though none of us enjoy troubled times, they do offer us an opportunity to show our children that God is real. This is vitally important. It was the breakdown of this transfer of faith from one generation to the next that put Israel in a terrible spiritual condition in the time of the judges.

> And the people served the LORD all the days of Joshua, and all the days of the elders that outlived Joshua, who had seen all the great works of the LORD, that he did for Israel. And Joshua the son of Nun, the servant of the LORD, died, being an hundred and ten years old. And they buried him in the border of his inheritance in Timnathheres, in the mount of Ephraim, on the north side of the hill Gaash. And also all that generation were gathered unto their fathers: and there arose another generation after them, which knew not the LORD, nor yet the works which he had done for Israel. And the children of Israel did evil in the sight of the LORD, and served Baalim: And they forsook the LORD God of their fathers, which brought them out of the land of Egypt, and followed other gods, of the gods of the people that were round about them, and bowed themselves unto them, and provoked the LORD to anger.—JUDGES 2:7–12

Many years ago when my daughter Karissa was probably three or four years old, we moved to a new home that didn't have a swimming pool as our old one had. We got her a little three foot pool to splash around in and play. One night I was out jogging, and I felt impressed to ask God to do something that would obviously be from Him. We didn't have to have a pool; it wasn't a need, but I felt led to pray for one. I didn't tell anyone else; I just started praying. A few days later Karissa asked about us getting an in-ground pool. I said, "Why don't we pray about it together?"

We prayed about getting a pool every day. After a little time went by, I was preaching at a church in Georgia. There was a man in that church who owned a swimming pool company. We talked about his business a little bit, and he told me that they had an above-ground pool that a school had planned to use for a giveaway, but there had been a change in plans and he was left with it. He made me a great offer on it, but that wasn't what Karissa and I had been praying for so I didn't say yes. He walked away, and then stopped and came back. "Have you ever thought about putting in an in-ground pool?" he asked. "Yes, I have!" I said.

He brought his crew up from Georgia to install the pool he sold me for about one third of the normal price. We enjoyed that pool together. Nearly every time we went swimming, I would ask Karissa, "Why do we have a pool?" "Because God gave it to us," she would reply. Have your kids ever seen God answer your prayers? The widow's sons watched a miracle unfold before their eyes—a miracle they were part of by helping to gather the vessels and then carrying them to the mother as she was pouring out the oil.

Let me remind you of this important part of the story that highlights the nature of faith. Elisha did not perfectly explain what was going to happen. He told her to gather vessels and pour her oil into them, but he didn't give her a lot of detail. Faith is acting according to God's Word whether or not we understand how things will work out. Many times God does not explain in detail what His plans are. We will never understand many things until we get to Heaven. While you're walking in faith, be sure you have plenty of empty vessels. If God is going to bless something, make sure He has lots to bless. Use what you have and trust Him to make it enough.

GOD'S ACCOMPLISHMENT

Elisha told the widow to take the oil that she had and use it to fill the vessels. God likes for us to be dependent on Him. All of the credit, all of the honor, all of the glory for everything we accomplish belongs to Him. If we need Him, we pray more. If we need Him, we trust more. If we need Him, we glorify Him more. God does what we cannot do for ourselves.

Notice first *the extent of the miracle.* The widow's little pot of oil filled every vessel they had borrowed. She received exactly as much oil as she had faith to bring in vessels. There was no more and no less. If she had borrowed half as many vessels as she did, she would have ended up with half as much oil as she did. If she had borrowed twice as many vessels, she would have ended up with twice as much oil as she did.

Then notice *the exhortation after the miracle.* When she told Elisha what had happened, he told her to sell the oil, pay off her debts, and live on the amount that remained. There is a great deal of practical wisdom in doing what you can to get out of debt. But it is even more vital that we live within our means.

Finally we see *the effect of the miracle.* The widow was blessed and went into business. I don't think the Bible is meant as a textbook on government or economics, but it does contain principles we can see and should follow in our own lives and as a nation. The Bible supports hard work and enterprise. God's plan is not for the government to paternalistically meet every need of every citizen. Elisha could have just given the widow money to pay her debts; instead he gave her the opportunity to do something that would provide not just for the immediate need but for the future. She had to take the initiative and do the work, but it resulted in a wonderful provision.

The Bible teaches self-reliance and individual responsibility. Paul wrote, "...*if any would not work, neither should he eat*" (2 Thessalonians 3:10). Paul is not talking about people who can't work; he's talking about people who are able to work but are not willing to do so. You are not doing a favor to an unwilling person if you feed him. That simply enables and encourages bad behavior and ensures that it will continue.

We love the "unexpected check in the mail" stories. We love the "canceled debt" stories. We love the "brand new car parked in the driveway" stories. But God usually gives us the "go sell the oil" story. A wise man said the reason we don't recognize opportunity when it knocks on our door is because it's disguised in work clothes. God may not perform a miraculous, instantaneous work in your life. He told Moses that the process of Israel taking over the Promised Land would take time. "*I will not drive them out from before thee in one year; lest the land become desolate, and the beast of the field multiply against thee. By little and little I will drive them out from before thee, until thou be increased, and inherit the land*" (Exodus 23:29–30).

LIFE APPLICATIONS

We have a particular obligation to help God's people. Galatians 6:10 says, *"As we have therefore opportunity, let us do good unto all men, especially unto them who are of the household of faith."* Even if you only have a little, God wants you to help those who have less. This burdened widow came to Elisha with her desperate plea for help, and his response required her to both do some work herself and receive help from others.

Debt leads to bondage. Proverbs 22:7 says, *"The rich ruleth over the poor, and the borrower is servant to the lender."* Any time, but especially during troubled economic times, is a good time to decrease debt rather than increase it. Though some significant tax advantages are offered for having a mortgage, I am personally working to pay mine off early. I understand not everyone can do that, but there is enormous freedom in being unencumbered.

Even people in deep trouble must do what they can first. The concept of the "free lunch" is destructive to character and initiative. Remember, Moses instructed the children of Israel to leave the corners of their fields unharvested (Leviticus 19:9–10) so that the poor people could come and gather the food that remained. But they were not given it—they worked hard to get it. If you haven't done everything you can, God is not obligated to do more. What do you have in your house? Have you used it yet?

God wants us to focus on what we do have, not on what we don't. When I first came to First Baptist Church of Bridgeport we didn't have much. The building was a wreck. The attendance was small. But we did what we could with what we had. We went soulwinning. We ran buses. We fixed up the property. God blessed us, and the church grew. If we had focused on what we lacked, our church would never have grown. If you fix your attention on what is lacking, you may well miss God's provision when it comes.

Most of God's provision involves our effort. First Timothy 5:8 says, *"But if any provide not for his own, and specially for those of his own house, he hath denied the faith, and is worse than an infidel."* If you are short of money, pray; but don't just pray. Get a second job. Take advantage of every opportunity you have. The old farmer said, "The best place to pray for corn is at the end of the hoe handle."

Being in business is biblical. God put this widow in the oil business. During the Depression, my mother and grandmother made pies and cakes and went door to door selling them. When Paul was traveling as a missionary, he received occasional gifts from churches, but he paid most of his expenses himself by working as a tentmaker (Acts 18:3). Be willing to take initiative and work to make things better for yourself and your family.

EIGHT

The Reluctant Widow

And the word of the LORD came unto him, saying, Arise, get thee to Zarephath, which belongeth to Zidon, and dwell there: behold, I have commanded a widow woman there to sustain thee. So he arose and went to Zarephath. And when he came to the gate of the city, behold, the widow woman was there gathering of sticks: and he called to her, and said, Fetch me, I pray thee, a little water in a vessel, that I may drink. And as she was going to fetch it, he called to her, and said, Bring me, I pray thee, a morsel of bread in thine hand. And she said, As the LORD thy God liveth, I have not a cake, but an handful of meal in a barrel, and a little oil in a cruse: and, behold, I am gathering two sticks, that I may go in and dress it for me and my son, that we may eat it, and die. And Elijah said unto her, Fear not; go and do as thou hast said: but make me thereof a little cake first, and bring it unto me, and after make for thee and for thy son. For thus saith the LORD *God of Israel, The barrel of meal shall not waste, neither shall the cruse of oil fail, until the day that the* LORD *sendeth rain upon the earth. And she went and did according to the saying of Elijah: and she, and he, and her house, did eat many days. And the barrel of meal wasted not, neither did the cruse of oil fail, according to the word of the* LORD, *which he spake by Elijah.*—1 KINGS 17:8–16

During the wicked reign of Ahab, God raised up the prophet Elijah to speak the truth. Elijah told the king that because of the Baal worship Ahab and Jezebel had encouraged among the people, there would be a great drought in the land. Elijah told Ahab that it would not rain until he said it would rain. Of course that message wasn't popular, and Elijah had to flee for his life.

Once the rain stopped, it wasn't long until people started getting hungry. The ground dried up, the crops died, and food was hard to come by. God had commanded Elijah to go and hide by a brook named Cherith. That took care of his need for water, and God instructed ravens to bring Elijah food. Now if you know anything about ravens, you know they wouldn't be your first choice for a waiter, but God was providing for his prophet. As more time passed without rain, the brook began to dry up, and that is where we begin the story of the reluctant widow.

THE REVELATION

God directed the steps of Elijah. He told him exactly where to go. He told Elijah to "dwell there" in Zarephath. Now on the surface this advice makes no sense. Zarephath was not in Israel; it was in Zidon. If there was one person on Earth who wanted Elijah dead more than Ahab, it was Jezebel, and Zidon was her home country. In fact, her father Ethbaal was king over Zidon. If they had a version of "Zidon's Most Wanted" in those days, Elijah's picture would have led every broadcast. He was public enemy number one.

In addition, it seems likely that the widow to whom God sent Elijah was also a Baal worshipper. When Elijah gave her the message that the God of Israel said that she was to provide food for him, she responded by talking about "The LORD *thy* God." It was not until the end of the story that she declared that Elijah was God's man and that his words were true.

God not only sent Elijah to a pagan place, but He sent Elijah to stay with a widow. Imagine an evangelist coming to your town, not for a week long meeting but for a couple of years, who needs a place to stay. Now imagine God telling him to go live with a poor widow in the church. It doesn't make sense. Yet God had a purpose and plan in mind. God told Elijah that He "had commanded" that widow to sustain him during the famine. I believe from the way the story reads that God told the widow that Elijah was coming. She didn't act at all surprised when he showed up at the gates of the city. She wasn't thrilled at doing the task, but she did it.

God commanded this woman to take care of Elijah. In our understanding, we would expect Elijah to take care of the widow. That wasn't God's plan. Sometimes God puts us in the position of depending on those we would rather not depend on.

It reminds us that we are not the source of our provision and sustenance; He is.

THE RELUCTANCE

When Elijah got to Zarephath, he met the widow at the gate of the city. We are not told how Elijah recognized her as the one to whom God had sent him. I think the Spirit of God led him to her at a time when she was available to meet him. Elijah then petitioned the widow for help. He asked her first for a drink of water. Keep in mind that there was a severe drought, so asking for water was not a simple request. Though God had commanded her to help him, Elijah did not order her around; he requested water with, "I pray thee."

Then he asked her to bring back something for him to eat as well. Now, she responded with reluctance. She was literally down to the bottom of the barrel. She told Elijah she was going to gather two sticks to cook everything she had left. Now I don't know if you have ever built a campfire or a fire in a fireplace, but two sticks won't make much fire. I'm struck by her situation. She didn't say to Elijah, "I don't know what we're going to do." Instead she was preparing for certain death because of the famine. She was at the point of despair. She had no help, no hope, and she saw no way of escape.

Late in 1914, just as World War I was starting, Ernest Shackleton led an expedition to attempt to cross the entire continent of Antarctica. Early in 1915, disaster struck as their ship the *Endurance* was trapped in ice and later sank. The crew survived and remained in a hastily built camp for a while, and then took the ship's lifeboats which they had rescued to the desolate Elephant Island. Most of the crew remained there while Shackleton and five others took the largest lifeboat and made a desperate attempt to reach help.

After surviving a hurricane that sank many full-size ships, they finally reached the South Georgia Island and made their way across it. An explorer who retraced their steps some forty years later said, "I do not know how they did it, except they had to." In August of 1916, two years after they left England, the remaining crew was rescued and returned home to a hero's welcome. Though his mission to cross Antarctica had failed, Shackleton was recognized as a hero for his daring efforts to bring all of his men safely home.

Even when there seems to be no hope, keep on going.

THE REMINDER

I wonder how Elijah felt when he found out that the woman God had commanded to feed him didn't have any food. That would be pretty discouraging. I think I would have been tempted to say, "I'm sorry, I must have the wrong widow. I'll go look for somebody else." Instead Elijah said what may be the two most important words to remember in troubled times: "Fear not." What he is about to tell her is completely outlandish by human standards. He told her to feed him before feeding herself or even her son. But first, he encourages her.

God sent Elijah to the widow to be sustained. What Elijah told her, and what I'm telling you today is that regardless of the circumstances, regardless of the resources, regardless of what human reasoning says, you had better do God's will first. This principle is found throughout the Bible. *"Honour the LORD with thy substance, and with the firstfruits of all thine increase"* (Proverbs 3:9). *"But seek ye first the kingdom of God, and his righteousness…"* (Matthew 6:33). *"Upon the first day of the week let every one of you lay by him in store…"* (1 Corinthians 16:2). Even in difficult times, put God first.

Notice that Elijah not only reminded the widow of the priority, but he reminded her of a promise. Now the promise was not what I would have chosen. If I had been setting things up, I would have liked for it to have said, "If you feed Elijah first, the barrel of meal will be full and the cruse of oil will overflow." That is not what God said. Sometimes He blesses us abundantly. Other times He gives us just enough. Basically what Elijah said to her was, "You won't have any more, but you won't ever run out." That is a minimal promise—but it is enough to get you through any storm!

This miracle of God's provision was promised to last as long as the drought did. When the rain returned, the barrel of meal and the cruse of oil would no longer be refilled. God never promised to do what you can do for yourself. God prefers that we work. That is His plan. Many people would rather have God do the work so they can sit back and coast. He didn't promise to care for the widow forever—just until the famine passed.

God did exactly what He said He would do. He always does! The widow's food lasted "many days." She and her son and Elijah were provided for, a little bit at a time. That is usually how God works. By His grace, through means we cannot always understand or explain, He sustains us. My father never had much money. He is a very generous man, and when he saw people in need, he did what he could to help them. He also raised five children and helped put all of us through college. Somehow he always paid his bills and had a place to live and a car to drive. It would not have seemed that he could have made it, but he did. God is faithful. You may have to scrape the barrel every day and shake the cruse to get out the last drops of oil—but don't despair. There will be enough for tomorrow.

THE REVERSAL

If you had asked the widow on the day that Elijah showed up how things were, she probably would have said something like, "Well things can't get much worse." However, they were about to get much worse. God was providing for her day after day, but she still had not yet come to a position of faith and trust in Him. Then she was challenged even more. Her son got sick and died. She could have gone to Elijah and said, "You helped me before. Your God works miracles. Can you help me now?" That's not what she did. She got angry at Elijah. She asked, "What have I to do with thee?" She then accused Elijah of killing her son!

This was a sudden change. Sometimes it's easier to take trouble if we have time to prepare for it. If your company announces there will be layoffs in three months, you can begin to plan and prepare. It's different if you get an unexpected message that your job is gone that day. If a loved one has been sick for months, you are more prepared for them to die than if something happens suddenly. You don't expect to bury your children, so when her son died, the widow was blindsided.

She did not respond to that very well. Her first reaction was to blame Elijah. She said in effect, "I don't want to have anything to do with you. This is all your fault." If you view things logically, Elijah had kept her son alive for much longer than he would have lived if Elijah had not come with God's miracle of provision. Instead of being grateful for what she had received, she griped about what she had lost.

Although the Bible does not tell us exactly why, the widow felt guilty for something in her life. She asked if Elijah had come "to call my sin to remembrance." When something bad happens, it's common to assume we are being judged for something. Let me assure you of this: when God is chastising you for something, you will know it for sure. God corrects us for the purpose of changing our behavior, and we can't do that unless we know what needs changing. Not every storm, not every heartache, not every sickness, not every tragedy is the judgment of God.

Finally, she responded with grief. Her heart was broken over the loss of her son. Because I work as a volunteer chaplain with the police, on a number of occasions I have had to notify family members that someone has died. I have seen almost every response imaginable to bad news. I've seen tears. I've seen people almost pass out. I once even saw a father curse the dead body of his son who had killed himself. Sometimes grief comes out in anger, sometimes in withdrawal, and sometimes in near hysteria.

Elijah did not respond to her griping or her guilt, nor did he try to stop her from grieving. Instead he simply said, *"Give me thy son."* When Elijah first met her, he said, *"Fetch me water."* Then he said, *"Make me a little cake."* Now she obeys his instruction again. He did not say to her, "If you give me your son, God will raise him from the dead." Faith does not demand explanations before it obeys.

Elijah went to his room with the boy's body and talked to God. That is always the right thing to do in hard times. Elijah laid the boy on his bed and asked God for help. As far as we know from what is recorded in the Bible, no one had ever been raised from the dead before. Elijah did not have an example of what he was praying for that he could use to strengthen his faith. He couldn't say, "God you did this for so-and-so, now please do it for me." What Elijah did have was the confidence that nothing was impossible for God. So he cried out to God for help. God heard the prayer of Elijah, and the boy's soul returned to his body as he came back to life.

THE REALIZATION

I am fascinated by what the widow said to Elijah, *"Now by this I know that thou art a man of God, and that the word of the LORD in thy mouth is truth"* (1 Kings 17:24). The miraculous provision she had received had not brought her to this point of faith, but the raising of her son from the dead did. Sometimes we lose patience with people when they don't get things right away. We may think they should have already "gotten it," but God knows when someone needs to learn a lesson. When she held her son who had been brought back to life, the widow acknowledged God's truth. Here are a few lessons we need to remember from this wonderful story.

When we give to God first, He makes what's left enough. God does not promise to make you rich. He does make some people rich but not everyone. He does promise to supply what we need. The Bible tells us over and over again that God must be in first place. If you are in trouble, do not pull back on what you are doing for God. Don't stop giving, praying, going to church, or witnessing. You need His help more than ever.

Much of God's provision is more impressive in retrospect. Because of the day-to-day nature of God replenishing her supplies, I don't think the widow was blown away by what happened. Looking back, it looks like a bigger miracle than it did at the time. It's important to try to appreciate what God is doing while it's happening.

God usually uses ordinary people and ordinary means to sustain His work. God didn't provide the widow an oil well, He just gave her enough for each day. God can and does still work miracles, and we have every right to ask for His help with our struggles. However, instead of sitting back and waiting for Him, we need to be actively involved in doing everything we know to do.

God's provision should convince us of His love and care. We can convince ourselves that because we're having hard times it means that He has abandoned us. Look back at all He has done for you through the years and let that strengthen your faith.

Things usually can and often do get worse. I read somewhere this statement: "They said smile; things could get worse. I smiled, and sure enough they did." Jesus said, *"Sufficient unto the day is the evil thereof"* (Matthew 6:34). That doesn't mean there will be no trouble tomorrow; it means there will be. We sometimes adopt the American attitude that things are always supposed to be nice and comfortable. That is not God's promise.

When things do get worse, God is still able. When the widow's son died, she lost whatever confidence she had built up from daily provision of her needs. Most of us have limits to our faith. As long as we can figure out how things could work, we're confident. But when we reach the point where we don't see any way out, we need to believe God anyhow. All of God's dealings with us are intended to increase our faith. If we don't learn the lesson, we may have to repeat the class; that's not a pleasant experience. Learn the lesson of the reluctant widow and trust Him no matter what. God loves you, and He will provide for all of your needs.

NINE

Why Art Thou Cast Down?

As the hart panteth after the water brooks, so panteth my soul after thee, O God. My soul thirsteth for God, for the living God: when shall I come and appear before God? My tears have been my meat day and night, while they continually say unto me, Where is thy God? When I remember these things, I pour out my soul in me: for I had gone with the multitude, I went with them to the house of God, with the voice of joy and praise, with a multitude that kept holyday. Why art thou cast down, O my soul? and why art thou disquieted in me? hope thou in God: for I shall yet praise him for the help of his countenance. O my God, my soul is cast down within me: therefore will I remember thee from the land of Jordan, and of the Hermonites, from the hill Mizar. Deep calleth unto deep at the noise of thy waterspouts: all thy waves and thy billows are gone over me. Yet the LORD will command his lovingkindness in the

daytime, and in the night his song shall be with me, and my prayer
unto the God of my life. I will say unto God my rock, Why hast
thou forgotten me? why go I mourning because of the oppression of
the enemy? As with a sword in my bones, mine enemies reproach
me; while they say daily unto me, Where is thy God? Why art thou
cast down, O my soul? and why art thou disquieted within me?
hope thou in God: for I shall yet praise him, who is the health of
my countenance, and my God.—PSALM 42:1–11

Though we are not told for certain, many Bible students
believe that Psalm 42 and 43 were written by King Hezekiah.
They definitely match the pattern of trouble and response that
we read about in the accounts of his life. While Hezekiah was a
good king over God's people, that did not stop him from having
problems. Some people seem to think that God owes them a
free ride—that nothing should ever go wrong in their lives. That
might be a nice way to live (although it probably wouldn't be
good for our character), but that is not what the Bible teaches
about life. Jesus said, *"in the world ye shall have tribulation"*
(John 16:33).

That was true during the reign of Hezekiah. Hezekiah
faced two major challenges—an invasion and an illness. First
he had to deal with the Assyrian army under Sennacherib, an
overwhelming force that invaded his kingdom. Later he faced
a life-threatening illness. In each occasion, Hezekiah turned
to God and sought His help. As we look at Hezekiah's life, we
see several principles that can help us when we face times of
difficulty, trouble, discouragement, and distress.

HEZEKIAH'S DEDICATION

*Now it came to pass in the third year of Hoshea son of
Elah king of Israel, that Hezekiah the son of Ahaz king
of Judah began to reign. Twenty and five years old was
he when he began to reign; and he reigned twenty and
nine years in Jerusalem. His mother's name also was
Abi, the daughter of Zachariah. And he did that which
was right in the sight of the LORD, according to all that
David his father did. He removed the high places, and
brake the images, and cut down the groves, and brake
in pieces the brasen serpent that Moses had made: for
unto those days the children of Israel did burn incense
to it: and he called it Nehushtan. He trusted in the
LORD God of Israel; so that after him was none like him
among all the kings of Judah, nor any that were before
him. For he clave to the LORD, and departed not from
following him, but kept his commandments, which the
LORD commanded Moses. And the LORD was with him;
and he prospered whithersoever he went forth: and he
rebelled against the king of Assyria, and served him
not. He smote the Philistines, even unto Gaza, and the
borders thereof, from the tower of the watchmen to the
fenced city.—2 KINGS 18:1–8*

Hezekiah did not have the benefit of a godly father. Ahaz
was a weak and worldly king who ignored the advice of the
prophet Isaiah and allowed multiple false gods to be worshiped
in Israel. When Hezekiah came to the throne, he inherited a

small nation beset by divisions and filled with people who had turned away from God. Despite all this, he dedicated his heart fully to following God. It's important to note that Hezekiah started out right. Before the big troubles came, he was already following the godly pattern established by David. That prepared him to do right when the troubled times came to his kingdom and his life. Dr. Bob Jones, Sr. used to say, "Do right till the stars fall…and if the stars fall, still do right."

Hezekiah kept the commandments of God. Many of the kings of Israel and Judah did not, perhaps feeling that the rules were for the "little people." God's Word is mandatory. No matter who you are or what position you hold, you are responsible for obedience to the Bible. Hezekiah also focused on the spiritual. Many times when we're in seasons of trouble or difficulty, we seek material solutions first; instead Hezekiah turned to God first. Now having said that, we should not treat God like a genie in a bottle. He has no obligation to bail us out of trouble we got ourselves into by foolish or sinful actions. He may graciously choose to do so, but we should be living in obedience so that any troubles that come are not the result of our own conduct.

Notice also that Hezekiah was persistent. He did not just start out right; he kept on doing right. Have you ever known someone who went on a diet but quit after a couple of weeks? Maybe they got discouraged because they didn't lose weight fast enough, or they got bored with the food choices they were allowed. Whatever the reason, it is certain that if you don't stick to a diet you aren't going to lose weight. We have a society that is in love with quick fixes and instant cures, but the Christian life is a marathon rather than a sprint.

HEZEKIAH'S DETERMINATION

*And it came to pass, when king Hezekiah heard it, that he rent his clothes, and covered himself with sackcloth, and went into the house of the LORD. And he sent Eliakim, which was over the household, and Shebna the scribe, and the elders of the priests, covered with sackcloth, to Isaiah the prophet the son of Amoz. And they said unto him, Thus saith Hezekiah, This day is a day of trouble, and of rebuke, and blasphemy: for the children are come to the birth, and there is not strength to bring forth. It may be the LORD thy God will hear all the words of Rabshakeh, whom the king of Assyria his master hath sent to reproach the living God; and will reprove the words which the LORD thy God hath heard: wherefore lift up thy prayer for the remnant that are left. So the servants of king Hezekiah came to Isaiah. And Isaiah said unto them, Thus shall ye say to your master, Thus saith the LORD, Be not afraid of the words which thou hast heard, with which the servants of the king of Assyria have blasphemed me. Behold, I will send a blast upon him, and he shall hear a rumour, and shall return to his own land; and I will cause him to fall by the sword in his own land.—*2 KINGS 19:1–7

Hezekiah was facing an attack from an overwhelming enemy. There was no possible way for his forces to win. The Assyrians believed that because they had defeated other nations (including the northern kingdom of Israel) and their gods, that the God of Judah would be just another deity without the power to deliver those who worshiped Him. They didn't know who God was, but they were about to find out. That's because Hezekiah did what we should always do when we're in trouble— he turned to God for help.

He sent word to the prophet Isaiah to ask for counsel. Isaiah told Hezekiah not to be afraid. That's pretty tough advice to follow when you have a massive, armed enemy encamped outside your walls, or when you've just been laid off and don't know how you're going to pay the bills, or have received a life-threatening diagnosis from your doctor, or found out that one of your children has a major spiritual issue. Yet no matter how difficult it is, maintaining our faith and courage is crucial as we go through difficult times.

As the story continues, we find that things didn't get better right away. Though Isaiah promised that God would deliver His people, the messenger of Sennacherib returned with yet another threat. This threat was a direct attack on Hezekiah's confidence in God. The Assyrians listed a number of different gods they had defeated and warned Hezekiah not to trust in his God. Ever since the Garden of Eden, Satan has been attacking people's confidence in God's words, and that trend continues today. But notice how Hezekiah responded.

Second Kings 19:14 says, *"And Hezekiah received the letter of the hand of the messengers, and read it: and Hezekiah went up into the house of the LORD, and spread it before the LORD."* Hezekiah didn't go to his generals to ask them what they thought he should do; he didn't poll the population for their opinion on his response; he didn't seek out his counselors to figure out a way to bribe the Assyrians to go away. He went to God.

Hezekiah's prayer was very specific. He asked for God's deliverance, not to get him out of trouble, but for God's glory. Second Kings 19:19 says, *"Now therefore, O LORD our God, I beseech thee, save thou us out of his hand, that all the kingdoms of the earth may know that thou art the LORD God, even thou only."* God can work through your difficulties and times of trouble to bring honor and glory to His name—and that is more important than our comfort and ease. Don't spend all your time praying for escape; ask also that God will be glorified through your circumstances.

God heard that prayer and sent word through the prophet Isaiah that He would bring deliverance to Judah in such a way that no one would doubt that it was God who had delivered His people. At this point in history, the Assyrians had never lost a battle. They had never been forced to retreat before an enemy, but they had never faced God Almighty fighting for His people before either. God did exactly what He promised. (He always does.)

And it came to pass that night, that the angel of the LORD went out, and smote in the camp of the Assyrians an hundred fourscore and five thousand: and when they arose early in the morning, behold, they were all dead corpses. So Sennacherib king of Assyria departed, and went and returned, and dwelt at Nineveh. And it came to pass, as he was worshipping in the house of Nisroch his god, that Adrammelech and Sharezer his sons smote him with the sword: and they escaped into the land of Armenia. And Esarhaddon his son reigned in his stead.—2 KINGS 19:35–37

Hezekiah's army never had to unsheathe a sword, hurl a spear, or launch a single stone from a catapult. In fact, they didn't even have to wake up. One angel took care of the whole job in one night. The devil will tell you that your situation is impossible, but if you remain faithful, courageous, and committed, nothing is impossible. God can and will keep His promises to you. Too many times we give up and fail to see the victory, not because God was not able, but because we were not determined and committed. If you never go through a crisis, you will never see a miraculous deliverance. However, it is also true that doing the right thing does not guarantee that you will be popular.

HEZEKIAH'S DETRACTORS

And Hezekiah sent to all Israel and Judah, and wrote letters also to Ephraim and Manasseh, that they should come to the house of the LORD at Jerusalem, to keep the passover unto the LORD *God of Israel. For the king had taken counsel, and his princes, and all the congregation in Jerusalem, to keep the passover in the second month. For they could not keep it at that time, because the priests had not sanctified themselves sufficiently, neither had the people gathered themselves together to Jerusalem. And the thing pleased the king and all the congregation. So they established a decree to make proclamation throughout all Israel, from Beersheba even to Dan, that they should come to keep the passover unto the* LORD *God of Israel at Jerusalem: for they had not done it of a long time in such sort as it was written. So the posts went with the letters from the king and his princes throughout all Israel and Judah, and according to the commandment of the king, saying, Ye children of Israel, turn again unto the* LORD *God of Abraham, Isaac, and Israel, and he will return to the remnant of you, that are escaped out of the hand of the kings of Assyria. And be not ye like your fathers, and like your brethren, which trespassed against the* LORD *God of their fathers, who therefore gave them up to desolation, as ye see. Now be ye not stiffnecked, as your fathers were, but yield yourselves unto the* LORD, *and enter into his sanctuary, which he hath sanctified for ever: and serve the* LORD *your God, that the fierceness of his wrath may turn away from you. For if ye turn again unto the* LORD, *your brethren and your children shall find compassion before them that lead them captive, so that they shall come again into this land: for the LORD your God is gracious and merciful, and will not turn away his face from you, if ye return unto him. So the posts passed from city to city through the country of Ephraim and Manasseh even unto Zebulun: but they laughed them to scorn, and mocked them.*—2 CHRONICLES 30:1–10

Hezekiah was trying his best to do the right things. He was the best king the nation of Judah ever had. We see here that after he had repaired and restored the Temple, Hezekiah wanted the nation of Israel to celebrate the Passover. They had gotten out of the habit of doing what God told them to do; in fact, the Bible says they hadn't done it for a long time. You'll find that if you stop doing what you should do, it's easy for that to become normal, and before you know it you will be a long way from God.

When Hezekiah tried to encourage the people to do right, he ran into a lot of resistance. That doesn't come as a surprise to me. There will always be people who don't want to do right themselves and aren't happy about it if we do. When we face resistance for doing right, we have a choice to make. Some people blame God. They say things like, "I tried to do right and God didn't make it easy for me." I think you'll search a long time in the Scriptures before you find that promise. Some people blame society. They may say, "In an evil world like ours, it's too hard to do right." I don't think Daniel or Paul would be very impressed by that argument.

Bear Bryant told his football players, "The first time you quit, it's hard. But every time after that, it gets easier." Don't let hard times and opposition stop you from doing what you are supposed to do. Some of the people mocked Hezekiah and made fun of his plans—but he celebrated the Passover anyway. At times you may feel as though you are the only one who is doing right. In those moments remember two things: First, you're not the only one. When Elijah complained to God that he was the only faithful one left, God told him there were seven thousand more. Second, you can do right anyway. Even if you are mocked, derided, ridiculed, and rebuked for it, you can obey the Lord.

People who have gotten used to doing wrong aren't going to be happy if you do right. Your life becomes an unspoken rebuke to their behavior. The spiritual condition of Israel had fallen so far that they thought obedience to God's Word was a big joke. The spiritual condition of America today is about the same. But I have some good news for you. We're on the winning side! God gives us the victory—we are not fighting *for* victory, we're fighting *through* victory that has already been won. I've read the last chapter in the Book, and the good guys win. No matter what opposition you face, keep doing right.

HEZEKIAH'S DISEASE

In those days was Hezekiah sick unto death. And the prophet Isaiah the son of Amoz came to him, and said unto him, Thus saith the LORD, Set thine house in order;

for thou shalt die, and not live. Then he turned his face to the wall, and prayed unto the Lord, saying, I beseech thee, O Lord, remember now how I have walked before thee in truth and with a perfect heart, and have done that which is good in thy sight. And Hezekiah wept sore. And it came to pass, afore Isaiah was gone out into the middle court, that the word of the Lord came to him, saying, Turn again, and tell Hezekiah the captain of my people, Thus saith the Lord, the God of David thy father, I have heard thy prayer, I have seen thy tears: behold, I will heal thee: on the third day thou shalt go up unto the house of the Lord. And I will add unto thy days fifteen years; and I will deliver thee and this city out of the hand of the king of Assyria; and I will defend this city for mine own sake, and for my servant David's sake. And Isaiah said, Take a lump of figs. And they took and laid it on the boil, and he recovered. And Hezekiah said unto Isaiah, What shall be the sign that the Lord will heal me, and that I shall go up into the house of the Lord the third day? And Isaiah said, This sign shalt thou have of the Lord, that the Lord will do the thing that he hath spoken: shall the shadow go forward ten degrees, or go back ten degrees? And Hezekiah answered, It is a light thing for the shadow to go down ten degrees: nay, but let the shadow return backward ten degrees. And Isaiah the prophet cried unto the Lord: and he brought the shadow ten degrees backward, by which it had gone down in the dial of Ahaz.—2 Kings 20:1–11

What do you do when you get bad news? I'm not talking about something minor; I'm talking about seriously bad news. What would you do when told, "You have to move out of the house tomorrow," or "You don't have a job anymore"? How would you react if you were to come home and find your husband with a suitcase in each hand or a note from your wife saying she isn't coming back or your child saying, "I'm tired of your rules and restrictions. I'm going to go where I want and dress how I want and live like I want"? What would you do then?

Hezekiah got really bad news, and it was no rumor—it was a word from God. He could have said, "Well, I guess that's it. I'll just die." He could have felt sorry for himself and given up. He could have blamed God for letting him get sick after all he had done to restore the Temple and promote the worship of the true God. Instead Hezekiah cried out to God in prayer. God does not always choose to heal our bodies or restore our finances, but He is always able to. God knows no impossibilities. No matter how desperate your situation, no matter how dark and deep your trouble, when you cry out to God, you are going to the right source for a solution.

God heard Hezekiah's prayer and sent Isaiah back with a new message—a message of hope. Isaiah told the king what to do to get better, and then he said, "In three days you will be back in the house of God." This was a special blessing for Hezekiah, who had done so much to restore the Temple. Here we see a spiritual truth. God's people need to be in the house of God, fellowshipping with and encouraging and being encouraged by other believers. If you are trying to do right, there is no better place to be.

When you're in trouble, do what Hezekiah did—pour out your heart before the Lord. When others criticize you for doing right, tell it to Him. When others say it's your fault things aren't going right, tell it to Him. When things seem hopeless, tell it to Him. The wonderful hymn writer Elisha Hoffman pastored a church in Benton Harbor, Michigan, for a number of years. Once as he was counseling a distraught mother, nothing he said seemed to help or bring her comfort. Finally he said to her, "You must tell Jesus." A new light shone from her eyes, and she said, "Yes, I must tell Jesus." Hoffman went home that day and wrote these beautiful words:

> I must tell Jesus all of my trials,
> I cannot bear these burdens alone;
> In my distress He kindly will help me,
> He ever loves and cares for His own.

> I must tell Jesus all of my troubles,
> He is a kind, compassionate Friend;
> If I but ask Him He will deliver,
> Make of my troubles quickly an end.

> Tempted and tried I need a great Saviour,
> One who can help my burdens to bear;
> I must tell Jesus, I must tell Jesus:
> He all my cares and sorrows will share.

> What must I do when worldliness calls me?
> What must I do when tempted to sin?

I must tell Jesus, and He will help me
Over the world the vict'ry to win.

I must tell Jesus! I must tell Jesus!
I cannot bear my burdens alone;
I must tell Jesus! I must tell Jesus!
Jesus can help me, Jesus alone.

The greatest events of Hezekiah's life—his victory over the invading forces of the Assyrians and his healing from a terminal illness—were a direct result of prayer. When Hezekiah was in trouble, he ran to talk to God. He trusted in God's goodness and praised His name even before he received the answers to his prayers. He believed that God was able to meet his needs and solve his problems. As a result, God worked in a mighty and wonderful way in Hezekiah's life.

HEZEKIAH'S DESIRE

Whether or not Hezekiah wrote Psalm 42, it certainly expresses the desire of a heart for intimate fellowship and enjoyment of the presence of God. In the midst of distress, as he poured out his soul before the Lord, the psalmist expressed his desire to praise the Lord. As he considered the approaching end of his life, he didn't react as many of us would have done. Some people I know would lament that they couldn't see their grandchildren grow up. Others would wish for one more special trip with family and loved ones. Some of the guys in my church would probably say, "Deer season hasn't opened yet, and I won't get a deer this year!"

Hezekiah said, "I want to go back to the house of God." He hated the thought of not being able to worship and praise God with the people of God. Many people are confused about worship in our day. Some people think it means organ music and whispers; others think it requires swaying and clapping and guitars. Worship comes from two combined words that mean "kiss toward." Worship is simply directing affection and ascribing worth to God.

It's interesting to me that Hezekiah continued that desire even in the face of difficulties with his own people. I've known a lot of people over the years who stopped going to church because someone said something nasty about them or someone wouldn't talk to them. Some of Hezekiah's own people were discouraging him by asking, "Where is your God?" Hezekiah could have allowed that to take his focus off God; instead he said, "I will praise Him more."

I don't however want to paint a picture of Hezekiah that makes you think he was always on top of things. He did get to the point of discouragement and even despair. He said, "My soul is cast down." Those aren't victorious, triumphant words. May I remind you of this? Jesus knows what it is like to feel pain. He knows what it is like to be abandoned and betrayed by friends. He knows what it is like to do good for people and receive no thanks in return. When you are hurting and you go to Him and pour out your pain and even frustration, He says, "I understand."

Though Hezekiah felt overwhelmed, he was not overcome. When I read his response, I think of the words of the Apostle Paul in 2 Corinthians 4:8, *"We are troubled on every side, yet not distressed; we are perplexed, but not in despair; Persecuted, but not forsaken; cast down, but not destroyed."* Today we'd probably say, "We're down, but not out." Trouble and difficulty are a part of life, not a sign that God has forsaken us. Keep on doing right. Keep on praying. Keep on believing in Him. No matter how bad things get, God is still going to take care of you. When you are in trouble, look to Him. You may be discouraged, but you don't have to be cast down.

Jim Ryun was one of the greatest runners the world has ever seen. Many of the high school track records he set in the early 1960s still stand nearly fifty years later. He qualified for the 1964 Olympic Team while still in high school. In the 1968 Olympic Games in Mexico City, Ryun, despite having just recovered from mononucleosis, won the silver medal in the 1,500 meter race. He was expected to finally win the gold in Munich in 1972, but during a qualifying heat, he was tripped by another runner and crashed to the track. Ryun got back on his feet, and though the other runners were far ahead, he still finished the race.

When you stumble and fall, when you are cast down and feel like quitting, get up. Keep on running and finish your race. You may not receive a gold medal in this world, but when the Father says, "Well done, thou good and faithful servant," nothing else will matter.

TEN

In Every Thing
Give Thanks

Rejoice evermore. Pray without ceasing. In every thing give thanks: for this is the will of God in Christ Jesus concerning you. Quench not the Spirit. Despise not prophesyings. Prove all things; hold fast that which is good. Abstain from all appearance of evil.
—1 THESSALONIANS 5:16–22

Rudyard Kipling was one of the best-selling authors of his era. Later in his life, someone calculated that Kipling was making one hundred dollars for every word he wrote—even more money one hundred years ago than it would be now. A reporter interviewing Kipling pulled out a one hundred dollar bill from his pocket and said, "Give me a one hundred dollar word." With a twinkle in his eyes, Rudyard Kipling replied, "Thanks!" Truly that is a valuable word.

Thanksgiving did not start out as the holiday that kicks off the Christmas shopping season. It did not originate with the Pilgrims having a feast giving thanks to God for giving them an abundant harvest to prepare them for the coming winter. It didn't begin with the proclamations issued by George Washington and Abraham Lincoln calling on all Americans to set aside a special day to give thanks for the many blessings they enjoy. Thanksgiving began with God, and it is an attribute that should be present in the lives of all of God's children.

I read about a five-year-old boy who was asked to pray at Thanksgiving dinner. As he began to pray, he thanked God for the turkey. But he didn't stop there. He thanked God for the farmer who had grown the turkey. He thanked God for the farmer who had grown the feed for the turkey and the person who had brought the feed from that farmer to the turkey. Then he thanked God for the people that took the turkey to the store. Next he thanked God for the people who put it on the shelf at the store and the cashier who checked out his mother when she bought the turkey, and he thanked God for his mother cooking the turkey and for his father paying for the turkey. Finally, he paused for a moment and said, "Did I leave anybody out?" His younger brother said, "God." And the five year old said, "I was coming to Him next."

It's interesting to note that of the seven instructions in this brief section of Scripture, only one comes with an explanation. All of the rest stand as simple imperatives, but the instruction to give thanks provides a motivation—it is God's will for us to be thankful people. This is true not only during good times; we are also to be thankful during troubled times. If we know that thankfulness is God's will, then why is it so hard for us to express our gratitude? Some people may say they don't have much for which to be thankful, but if they honestly assess their situation they can easily find plenty for which to be thankful, regardless of how difficult their circumstances may be.

HINDRANCES TO THANKSGIVING

The first thing that keeps us from being thankful is sin. I've never yet known a person who was intentionally remaining in sin who was also thankful. The Scripture says that our iniquities separate us from God (Isaiah 59:2). I've seen plenty of sinners who were enjoying the short term pleasures of sin. I've seen them ride the adrenaline rush of "getting away with it" for a brief time. But I've never seen them be happy and thankful.

Sin can make you defensive, as it did with King Saul when he was confronted by Samuel after Saul failed to utterly destroy the Amalekites. Sin can make you defiant, as it did with Pharaoh who hardened his heart against Moses' demands to let the children of Israel go. Sin can leave you depressed, as it did with Peter after he denied the Lord three times. Sin can make you doubt, as it did with Sarah who laughed when God promised her a son in her old age. Sin can leave you distressed, as it did with David who suffered greatly for covering his sin with Bathsheba. But sin will never make you thankful.

Another hindrance to thankfulness is selfishness. In the last chapter we talked about Hezekiah's wonderful healing in answer to prayer. God not only gave Hezekiah victory over the Assyrian army, but he added fifteen years to Hezekiah's life after he was at the point of death. That's an amazing story, but it has a sad ending. After Hezekiah recovered, messengers from the King of Babylon came to see him. Hezekiah foolishly showed them everything in Jerusalem—his weapons, his treasures, and his family.

Isaiah came to Hezekiah and asked him what happened. When Hezekiah told him, the prophet rebuked the king. Isaiah told him bluntly that everything he had shown the Babylonian emissaries would be taken away. Even worse, Hezekiah's son, who was not yet born, would be taken as a eunuch. Notice Hezekiah's response, *"Then said Hezekiah unto Isaiah, Good is the word of the LORD which thou hast spoken. And he said, Is it not good, if peace and truth be in my days?"* (2 Kings 20:19).

Can you imagine a more selfish response? "As long as I'm okay, I don't care what happens later." That's not right. However, that was in keeping with Hezekiah's behavior after his healing. Though he had been a good king, his priorities got out of line, and he was totally focused on himself. Second Chronicles 32:25 says, *"But Hezekiah rendered not again according to the benefit done unto him; for his heart was lifted up: therefore there was wrath upon him, and upon Judah and Jerusalem."* Focusing on himself kept Hezekiah from being properly thankful for all that he had received.

Another thing that keeps us from being thankful is an abundance of stuff. America is such a wealthy country in comparison to the rest of the world. Two thirds of the people alive today have never used a telephone. How many phones do you have in your home? I remember when it was a big deal if one of your neighbors had a television. Most families in America have multiple televisions now. While there are people who go hungry, the biggest problem we have is not starvation, but people who are overweight.

We see this truth illustrated in the story of the rich young ruler who came to Jesus. Luke 18 tells the story of a man who wanted to follow Jesus until he found out what it would cost. Jesus tried to show him that he was a sinner in need of a Saviour, but this man protested that he had fully obeyed the law from the time he was young. That wasn't true, but he was convinced of it. So Jesus, knowing his heart, replied, *"Sell all that thou hast, and distribute unto the poor, and thou shalt have treasure in heaven: and come, follow me"* (Luke 18:22). You can't get to Heaven by selling your possessions and giving them away, but this command highlighted the heart problem that was keeping the rich ruler from recognizing his need for a Saviour.

The natural human tendency is to take credit for our blessings rather than giving praise and thanks to God. We easily fall into the trap of thinking we deserve good things; in truth, we deserve nothing but Hell. Every good thing we have is a gift from God. The ruler had many possessions, but they did not make him grateful; in fact, they left him sorrowful because he wasn't willing to part with them.

HELPS TO THANKSGIVING

In order to be thankful, it is important that we remember. Hezekiah failed to be thankful because he forgot the great benefits he had received from God. Psalm 40:2 tells us that God took us out of a horrible pit and set our feet on a rock. I've been saved for a long time, and I was saved at a young age before I had committed any "big" sins. But I was in a pit and headed straight for Hell before God saved me. I needed salvation, and nothing I could do could earn it. By God's grace alone I was saved, and I don't ever want to forget that. If I do, I will likely stop being thankful.

Nehemiah 9:17 says of the children of Israel, *"And refused to obey, neither were mindful of thy wonders that thou didst among them; but hardened their necks, and in their rebellion appointed a captain to return to their bondage: but thou art a God ready to pardon, gracious and merciful, slow to anger, and of great kindness, and forsookest them not."* I encourage people to take time on a regular basis to review the wonderful works God has done, both in the pages of Scripture and in their own lives as well. I want to be mindful of His wonders; it helps me be thankful.

Not only should we remember the things God has done for us in the past, but we should also remember our future prospects. As a child of God, I have Heaven to look forward to—as a gift of His grace. When life doesn't look so good, I still have eternity to look forward to. It's easy to be thankful when I realize all that is in store for me. It's interesting that the Hebrew word *yadah* can be translated as either *thanksgiving* or *confession.* Why be thankful? Because all the good things we have now and will have later are things we do not deserve.

In addition to remembering, it is helpful to refocus. Philippians 4:6–7 says, *"Be careful for nothing; but in every thing by prayer and supplication with thanksgiving let your requests be made known unto God. And the peace of God, which passeth all understanding, shall keep your hearts and minds through Christ Jesus."* If we're looking at our problems, it is hard to be thankful; when we're focused on God's promises and His provision, thanksgiving is a normal reaction.

Yes, we have the ability and the privilege to pour out our hearts before the Lord and tell Him when we are burdened and troubled. But we also need to give thanks, even before we are delivered, for the goodness of God toward us. As I refocus my mind, I don't just think about the mountain of bills and the modest amount of money I have to pay it. I don't think about all the uncertainty in our economy and in our nation or whether the recession may mean that something might happen to my job. I don't think about those health and family burdens that I carry. But I begin to think about the fact that I am a child of God, and I give thanks. The same God who has sustained me every step of my journey thus far will never leave me nor forsake me. When I remember all the times God has delivered me when I thought there was no help or hope, I refocus, and my whole outlook changes.

Another wonderful aid to thanksgiving is rejoicing. Rejoicing is commanded; in fact Philippians 4:4 says, *"Rejoice in the Lord alway.*" We may not feel like rejoicing, but we are supposed to do it anyway.

I don't like to exercise. I have a Nordic Track machine. I'm supposed to be on it for an hour, and when I'm on it, I hate all sixty minutes. Liking exercise doesn't have anything to do with its effectiveness. If I exercise, I stay healthy. We may not always feel like being thankful, but we will be glad we did what we are supposed to do. You'll be surprised at what rejoicing does to your heart.

On September 6, 1860, the steamship *Lady Elgin* carried hundreds of people from Milwaukee, Wisconsin, to Chicago to hear a presidential campaign speech by Stephen A. Douglas. During the return voyage, early in the morning of September 8, the *Lady Elgin* was struck by the schooner *Augusta*, which was running without lights. The badly damaged ship carried only two lifeboats for more than seven hundred passengers and crew. The wreck would prove to be the worst loss of life ever on Lake Michigan.

When the morning dawned, hundreds of survivors were clinging to the wreckage just off the shore from Chicago. A young student named Edward Spencer who was preparing for the ministry at the Garrett Biblical Institute repeatedly plunged into the water and risked his own life to save as many as he could. For over six hours, the courageous young man went into the water again and again until he had saved 17 people. The exertion broke Spencer's health, and even after he left the hospital, he never completely recovered. He spent the rest of his life as an invalid.

Later Spencer wrote a tract describing his experience and testified that he knew of at least 50 people who had trusted Christ through reading his story. On the twentieth anniversary of the shipwreck, a reporter found Edward Spencer and interviewed him. He asked Spencer what he remembered most about that night when he saved 17 lives. Seated in his wheelchair, Spencer paused for a moment and then said, "I remember that none of them ever came back to say thank you."

Dr. Bob Jones, Sr. said, "When gratitude dies on the altar of a man's heart, that man is well nigh hopeless." Romans 1:21 identifies the lack of thankfulness as one of the first steps on the road to reprobation. Are you thankful today regardless of your circumstances? Have you given praise and thanks to God for all He has done? *Thanks* truly is a one hundred dollar word, and it is even more valuable as a lifestyle.

ELEVEN

No Mas

And Ahab told Jezebel all that Elijah had done, and withal how he had slain all the prophets with the sword. Then Jezebel sent a messenger unto Elijah, saying, So let the gods do to me, and more also, if I make not thy life as the life of one of them by to morrow about this time. And when he saw that, he arose, and went for his life, and came to Beersheba, which belongeth to Judah, and left his servant there. But he himself went a day's journey into the wilderness, and came and sat down under a juniper tree: and he requested for himself that he might die; and said, It is enough; now, O LORD, take away my life; for I am not better than my fathers.
—1 KINGS 19:1–4

One of the most famous boxing matches in history took place on November 25, 1980, between Roberto Duran and Sugar

Ray Leonard. Five months earlier, Duran had defeated Leonard for the WBC Welterweight title. The rematch took place in New Orleans, Louisiana, before a huge crowd at the Superdome. In the first fight, Leonard had abandoned his trademark slashing, quick-moving style in an unsuccessful attempt to go toe-to-toe with the larger Duran. This time he used his superior speed and movement to befuddle Duran. Late in the eighth round, Duran turned his back to Leonard and said to the referee, "No mas"— Spanish for "no more." Leonard was declared the victor by TKO and regained his title when Duran quit.

Elijah had reached the same point of defeat and desperation that Roberto Duran did. He told God, "I've had enough." He just couldn't take any more. He felt that he had served and struggled long enough, and he wanted to die. That is a depressing place to be. Why was this great and powerful prophet of God so discouraged? The answer to that question will help us deal with the hard times we face in our own lives.

THE REASON FOR DISCOURAGEMENT

It's ironic that the story of Elijah's depression doesn't begin with bad news; in fact it begins with good news and a great victory. Elijah confronted King Ahab for his wickedness and pronounced God's judgment on the land. After more than three years without rain, when Israel was in the grip of a terrible drought, Elijah returned to face Ahab again. A confrontation was arranged on Mt. Carmel between Elijah and 450 prophets of Baal and 400 prophets of the groves. They would each pray for fire to fall from Heaven so that the people could judge who truly was God.

Ahab accepted the challenge. After the false prophets prayed all day long with no response, crying out and even cutting themselves, Elijah offered a simple prayer of just sixty-three words, and fire fell from Heaven. After Elijah killed all the false prophets, he prayed, and God sent a torrential rain to break the drought. The people acknowledged that Jehovah was the only true God. Things were going great. It was at that moment that things started to fall apart for Elijah.

Elijah had seen a tremendous revelation of God's power. He had also seen a temporary response from God's people. Though they proclaimed that Jehovah was God, they were not ready to really give up their idol worship. This was not a permanent revival. The Bible doesn't tell us, but I think Elijah must have expected something more—a more lasting result.

That was followed by a total rejection of God's prophet. Jezebel did not come to Mt. Carmel, and when Ahab returned and told her what had happened, she was furious. She had done much to bring Baal worship to Israel, and she wasn't going to give up without a fight. She sent a message to Elijah that he had less than twenty-four hours to live. Elijah was a wanted man. In his complaint to God in 1 Kings 19:10, he said, *"they seek my life, to take it away."* As a result, Elijah said, "No mas."

We should not expect to be popular if we stand for the Word of God in a heathen world. At one time in his life Charles

Spurgeon was the most famous and most followed preacher in the world. His sermons "Morning and Evening" were printed in the secular newspapers. While the auditorium seated five thousand, he asked the members of the church to stay home on Sunday evenings so that lost people could find a place to sit and hear the Gospel. They used tickets to control entry because there was such a demand for seats.

At times he preached to crowds in excess of twenty thousand. He started a college to train preachers and ran several orphanages. Toward the end of his life, the group of churches he had been associated with, called the Baptist Union, began drifting away from the truth. Charles Darwin had proposed the theory of evolution, and many of these preachers tried to accommodate the Bible to fit in with these "scientific" discoveries. Spurgeon resisted that trend and called for a statement of faith that would be required for membership in the Baptist Union.

Spurgeon was no longer respected as he had once been. His health was declining, and he was struggling with kidney disease, gout, and rheumatism that would lead to his death at just fifty-seven years of age. Friends turned against him, and even many of those who had trained in his school refused to support his stand for the truth. In fact, Spurgeon's position in support of a basic statement of faith from Baptist pastors received just seven votes. You may face days when you have to stand alone. The temptation in those days is to give up and say, "No mas." Don't give up!

THE RESULTS OF DISCOURAGEMENT

Because Elijah was discouraged, he ran into the desert and crawled under a juniper bush and prayed to die. Juniper bushes grow low to the ground. To get under one, you have to get down incredibly low. Elijah was there because *he had a problem with following*. After Elijah gave God's message to Ahab, he was told to go to the brook Cherith. After a while, the brook dried up and God told him to go to Zarephath and stay with a widow. When the time was right, God told Elijah to go back to Israel and face Ahab. Elijah did all those things according to the Word of the Lord. Who told Elijah to run and hide? Jezebel. He stopped listening to God and started listening to people.

This story from Elijah's life shows us the danger of not following God. Psalm 32:8 says, *"I will instruct thee and teach thee in the way which thou shalt go: I will guide thee with mine eye."* God makes it His job to tell us what to do. If you know God has told you to do something, keep doing it until He tells you to do something else. You don't have to have peace to stay; you have to have peace to move. Don't take matters into your own hands. If you do, you're likely to end up discouraged.

It is not always wrong to move. Sometimes God wants you to go from one place to another. It is wrong to move just because you don't like the way things are going where you are. Even if a Jezebel is after you, she can't kill you. If you are in the will of God, you cannot die until it is His time for you to die. When that time does come, you don't want to miss it.

Elijah also had a problem with his feelings. A prayer to die isn't one that we see very often in the Bible. I don't believe Elijah was making a sincere request. If he had really wanted to die, he could have just stayed where he was and let Jezebel take care of the job. He was just desperate and discouraged and looking for help. Elijah had given in to his feelings. He bragged on himself to God and complained that he was the only one who was doing right.

To highlight the problem, God twice asked Elijah the same question, *"What doest thou here?"* If you look at 1 Kings 19:10 and 14, you'll see that Elijah gave Him the same answer each time. When I counsel with people and they keep repeating their complaints over and over again, that's usually a pretty good indication that they've been thinking about it a lot. When you rehearse your feelings over and over, you are on the path to the juniper bush of discouragement. Elijah was having a pity party.

Finally, Elijah had a problem with fellowship. The Bible tells us that Elijah left his servant in Beersheba. Jesus purposefully sent out the disciples two by two. It's good to have someone to encourage you. Solomon wrote, *"Two are better than one; because they have a good reward for their labour. For if they fall, the one will lift up his fellow: but woe to him that is alone when he falleth; for he hath not another to help him up"* (Ecclesiastes 4:9–10). Usually in the plan and providence of God there are fellow-helpers for your work.

Elijah's servant didn't get discouraged and quit. He didn't decide to switch sides and join the enemy. He wasn't laid off because of a bad economy. He got dumped because Elijah wanted to be alone. It is a warning sign when you don't want to be around God's people. Withdrawing from fellowship is a symptom of trouble. When you want fellowship the least, you probably need it the most.

Elijah's relationship with God wasn't what it should have been either. Instead of talking *to* God, even when he was in the presence of God, he talked *about* God. First Kings 19:10 says, *"And he said, I have been very jealous for the LORD God of hosts."* The natural thing to say would have been, "I have been very jealous for You." Almost always when people withdraw from human fellowship, they withdraw from Divine fellowship as well.

THE RESPONSE TO DISCOURAGEMENT

God gave comfort to Elijah in his discouragement. He sent an angel to prepare food for Elijah, and then Elijah rested. When he woke up, the angel fed him again, and his physical strength was restored. I think it's fair to say that part of Elijah's problem with depression was physical—he was exhausted after his efforts to turn the people back to God. Someone said, "Tired is stupid." I'm not sure that's exactly right, but getting proper rest, exercise, and food is invaluable, and that is especially true when we are discouraged.

I also think it's fair to say that the biggest problem Elijah had was spiritual. More than anything else, what Elijah needed was a new level of closeness to God. When Elijah heard the still, small voice, he came out of the cave where he was hiding (that's a pretty good metaphor for discouragement) and talked to God. You're not likely to get over your discouragement until you come out of your cave.

The method of communication God chose required Elijah to come out of hiding. You can observe a whirlwind or an earthquake or a fire from a distance, but you have to be close to hear a quiet voice. The Hebrew word for *still* means "whisper," and the word for *small* means "emaciated." God was drawing Elijah to Himself by the manner in which He spoke. Sometimes we don't hear the voice of God because we're still hiding in the cave. We want to see God's great power; instead He may choose to whisper to us so that we have to focus intently and draw close to Him. We are always in the presence of God, but sometimes we are not aware of it.

Jeremiah wrote these words to the people in captivity in Babylon: *"Then shall ye call upon me, and ye shall go and pray unto me, and I will hearken unto you. And ye shall seek me, and find me, when ye shall search for me with all your heart"* (Jeremiah 29:12–13). Sometimes trouble comes into our lives because God wants us to seek His presence. When we come to the place where God is all we have, we find that He is all we need.

I went to preach in a church in Illinois, and the pastor picked me up at the airport. As we drove to his city, he told me that his mother, his mother-in-law, and his son's mother-in-law had all just learned that they only had a short time to live. Each was suffering a very advanced stage of cancer. I did the best I could to be an encouragement to him, but I felt as though my words were inadequate to what he was facing. Often the only real help we find is in God.

It's interesting to me that God did not accept Elijah's complaint. He did not offer any sympathy to the griping prophet. He simply gave Elijah a set of instructions to carry out. Elijah was to go and anoint the future leaders of Syria and Israel, and then select Elisha to fill his office as prophet to the nation. God basically told him, "It's time to get back to work." God gave Elijah a commission and a companion to overcome his discouragement.

Notice also that God pointed out the flaw in Elijah's thinking. Elijah complained that he was the only one still serving God, but God told him that there were seven thousand more. Circumstances are never as bad as we think they are. God has a purpose and a plan that goes far beyond our lives. It was going on before we got here, and it will go on after we're gone. We are not the center of the world. What we can see and observe is only a tiny fraction of what God is doing.

Dr. Tom Malone founded the Emmanuel Baptist Church in Pontiac, Michigan, while he was still a student at what was then Bob Jones College in Cleveland, Tennessee. He would drive six hundred miles each way every weekend. Even today that would be about a ten hour drive, but in those pre-interstate days it took even longer. The church didn't have any money, so he personally signed the loan to buy their property. He helped the mason lay the bricks for their first building. In time, the church grew to more than 3,500 people.

When he was in his 70s, Dr. Malone retired. Under his successors the church went down and down and down. The few members who were still left called Dr. Malone and asked if he would come back. The first Sunday he preached, there were 90 people there. Someone asked if he wanted to rope off the empty pews in the large auditorium, and he replied, "We're going to face these empty pews until we fill them." The church began to grow again—in fact, for a period of time, they were the fastest growing church in the state of Michigan!

They were still having enormous financial difficulties from the decline of the previous several years. I heard him tell the story of sitting at his desk in the office surrounded by bills they couldn't pay. At an age when most people would say he should have been taking it easy, he was struggling to help a once-great church. He said, "That's it. I've had enough." He left the office and drove to a neighborhood and started going door to door sharing the Gospel. He witnessed to a lady and led her to Christ. He said, "By the time I got back to the office, I couldn't remember what my problems were!"

Sometimes the best thing to do when you are discouraged is to simply get back to work. Not everything will be accomplished in your lifetime, but God has a long frame of reference. He told Elijah that Hazael would bring the sword of justice to some, and Jehu would get others, and that Elisha would take care of anyone who escaped those two. In his poem "Retribution," Longfellow wrote, "The mills of God grind slowly, yet they grind exceeding small." You don't have to make sure everything turns out right; that is His job. You simply need to refuse to let discouragement derail you. Eat and rest, draw close to God once more, and then return to doing His purpose for your life.

TWELVE

Think It Not Strange

Beloved, think it not strange concerning the fiery trial which is to try you, as though some strange thing happened unto you: But rejoice, inasmuch as ye are partakers of Christ's sufferings; that, when his glory shall be revealed, ye may be glad also with exceeding joy. If ye be reproached for the name of Christ, happy are ye; for the spirit of glory and of God resteth upon you: on their part he is evil spoken of, but on your part he is glorified. But let none of you suffer as a murderer, or as a thief, or as an evildoer, or as a busybody in other men's matters. Yet if any man suffer as a Christian, let him not be ashamed; but let him glorify God on this behalf. For the time is come that judgment must begin at the house of God: and if it first begin at us, what shall the end be of them that obey not the gospel of God? And if the righteous scarcely be saved,

where shall the ungodly and the sinner appear? Wherefore let them that suffer according to the will of God commit the keeping of their souls to him in well doing, as unto a faithful Creator.
—1 PETER 4:12–19

The case Peter lays out here in his epistle is not really a happy one. It isn't about finding your "best life now" but rather about expecting fiery trials. Nero was on the throne in Rome, and his persecution against Christians was increasing. Being a committed Christian in those days was a risky proposition. Many perished for their faith. The people to whom Peter was writing needed help and encouragement, and Peter tells them to expect more trouble.

We have things that irritate us—things that make us say or think, "That's not fair." I returned from a preaching trip recently, and as I was pulling out of the airport, the parking lot attendant said, "Your tire is low." I looked and sure enough it was. So I drove very slowly to a gas station nearby and pumped it up. I had to pay 75 cents—imagine paying for air! It was cold outside, and it seemed as if it took forever for the tire to get full enough to drive home safely. No child of God should ever have to endure such suffering! Surely my reward in Heaven will be great. Well, I don't think the people Peter was writing would be very impressed with the scope of my problems, but in reality, we all do have things both large and small that are trials and hardships in our lives. The question is: how will we respond to them?

A PRECAUTION

First, Peter says that we should not think of the trials we experience as strange. *He tells us that trials are inevitable.* He doesn't say the fiery trial *might* come; he says it *is* going to come. Jesus said, *"In the world ye shall have tribulation"* (John 16:33). You are going to have troubles and trials and heartaches. You will be mistreated and misunderstood. You will make trips to the hospital and the cemetery. The doctor may tell you it's stage four cancer. You may get a knock on the door from a policeman. Trouble will come. The right question is not, "Why is this happening to me?" but "Why not me?" We have the privilege of living in America with great religious and economic freedom, but that is no guarantee against trouble.

Not only are trials inevitable, but we can also expect them to be intense. A fiery trial is not just a figure of speech—Christians were being burned alive by Nero in Rome. These trials are part of the Christian life. We do not receive a "get out of suffering free" card when we are saved. Fire refines metal. It melts away impurities and leaves only what is precious. Trials are designed to strengthen us. If we respond properly through trials, we will draw closer to God.

Be careful how you react when your trials come. Many people walk away from God, blaming Him for something He told them was going to happen. Many people withdraw from church, leaving behind the friends that would console them. Many people fall into bitterness because things didn't turn out the way they thought things should.

THE PRESCRIPTION

The first thing we are told to do when fiery trials come is to rejoice. Rejoicing in trials is built on faith that God will provide everything we need. The first time this Greek word is used in the Bible is in the story of the wise men who came from the east to see the King of the Jews. The song is wrong. They didn't follow the star across the desert. They made their trip because they saw the star, but they didn't see it again until they left Herod on their way to Bethlehem. Then it reappeared, and they followed it to the house where Jesus was. The Bible says, *"When they saw the star, they rejoiced with exceeding great joy"* (Matthew 2:10). Our rejoicing is not because of the trial but because we know God is faithful, even in trials, and so we calmly accept what comes.

We rejoice because we are taking part in the suffering of Jesus Christ. Peter wasn't just writing these words theoretically; he had already practiced what he was preaching when the church was being persecuted in Jerusalem. *"And to him they agreed: and when they had called the apostles, and beaten them, they commanded that they should not speak in the name of Jesus, and let them go. And they departed from the presence of the council, rejoicing that they were counted worthy to suffer shame for his name"* (Acts 5:40–41). When you suffer for Jesus, you are in extremely good company.

Years ago when I was a youth pastor, the pastor for whom I worked had cancer surgery. I went to visit him in the hospital, and the first thing he did was show me the scar. Why do we do that? It's a mark of something we went through and survived. It's a sign of the battle we went through.

Then Peter reminds us of what is coming. He talks about the revelation of the glory of Christ. If we had nothing to look forward to, trials would be unbearable. Peter says that when He appears, we will be glad with "exceeding joy." This is a different concept from the word *rejoice* at the beginning of verse 13. This word literally means to "jump for joy." If you can take the trials now, you're going to celebrate later on.

Notice that the Scripture says we are to rejoice "inasmuch" as we are taking part in the suffering of Jesus. That word does not mean "because" or "for the reason of" but rather "to the degree of" or "according to." The idea here is that our rejoicing is in accordance with the degree that we partake of Christ's sufferings. The more you suffer now, the more you will be blessed and rejoice later.

THE PROMISE

There is a difference in the reproach we receive because of bad behavior and the reproach we receive "for the name of Christ." I pass out tracts all the time. Not everybody takes one. On rare occasions, I've even had someone be nasty to me about it. I haven't endured persecution, but I have been reproached for presenting the Gospel.

Years ago, I was asked to witness to a man. When I visited his home and talked to him, I could tell he was under conviction, but he declined when I asked him to accept Christ. As I was backing out of the driveway, he came running out. "Can you pray that prayer with me? I really need God," he said. He started coming to church, and after a few weeks he asked me to witness to some of his friends. I walked up and said, "I'm Pastor Ouellette from First Baptist Church…." Immediately one of the men said, "What in the world happened to Ralph?" "What do you mean?" I asked. "Ralph won't drink anymore. He won't smoke anymore. He won't dance anymore. He says it's against the church rules," the man replied. Ralph was catching a little bit of grief from his friends because of the changes he had made in his life after his salvation. That is a good kind of reproach.

That kind of reproach should make us happy. Why? Because when we suffer for taking a stand for what is right, God then gives us grace, glory, strength, and help to bear it. The first martyr of the church was Stephen. Acts 7 records his sermon to the Jewish council. He gave them a history lesson of the Jewish people. When he began to apply the truth and the lessons of history to their current situation, they were enraged. They were so angry and under such conviction that they literally started biting him.

The Bible says that as Stephen looked up into Heaven, he saw Jesus standing at the right hand of God. That's interesting because the Bible tells us three times in the book of Hebrews that Jesus is seated at the right hand of God. I believe He stood up to welcome Stephen home. They stoned Stephen to death. His dying prayer echoed the words of Jesus on the cross, *"Lord, lay not this sin to their charge"* (Acts 7:60). At the time of his suffering and death, God's grace and glory rested on Stephen. When you need help most, God will be there for you.

THE PROHIBITION

Notice the contrast Peter draws between the causes of the right and wrong kinds of reproach. No believer should suffer because he is doing wrong and breaking the law. But if you do wrong and receive reproach, you deserve it. The list Peter gives us includes a surprising item. Most of us would say that being a busybody doesn't belong on the same list with murder, theft, and evildoing. When the Bible talks about being a busybody, it is referring to one who meddles with things that are none of his business.

It is right and appropriate to help people who are in trouble. It is wrong and reproachful to meddle in things that are none of your business. Proverbs 26:17 says, *"He that passeth by, and meddleth with strife belonging not to him, is like one that taketh a dog by the ears."* Not all meddling is motivated by bad desires; some people are genuinely trying to be helpful. But I often tell people, "Do not give unsolicited advice." Most of us have a full time job trying to make sure we do right ourselves without spending all day trying to straighten out others.

Some years ago a pastor who was having trouble in his church called me and asked for help. The former pastor had hand-picked this man as his successor and had stayed on in the church after his retirement. The new man hadn't done everything the same way, and the former pastor and his wife started stirring up trouble among the congregation. I was asked to come and moderate the business meeting where they would go through everything. I felt led to go because I thought I could be helpful to the people involved and the church, and I believe that I was. However that is not the reason I went. I agreed to go because they had asked for my help. If they hadn't invited me, I would have stayed out of it. I don't want to suffer as a busybody.

THE PURPOSE

Why does God bring suffering into our lives? To glorify Him. Suffering for right is not a disgrace; it is a demonstration of God's grace and God's power. One of the most powerful fictional books ever written was *Uncle Tom's Cabin*. Penned by the ardent abolitionist Harriet Beecher Stowe, it presented such a powerful portrayal of the evils and horrors of slavery that it helped push the nation toward ending it. First published in 1852, the book sold 300,000 copies in its first year in print. In fact, when Stowe met with President Abraham Lincoln, he is reported to have said, "So you are the little woman who wrote the book that started this great war."

In the book, the cruel slave owner Simon Legree finds out that one of the main characters, Uncle Tom, is a Christian when he finds Tom's hymnbook among his belongings. "Humph! Pious to be sure," Legree says. "You belong to the church?" "Yes, Mas'r," Tom said firmly. "Well, I'll soon have that out of you. I'm your church now! You understand—you've got to be as I say." Legree tries to get Tom to flog a woman who hadn't picked enough cotton to suit him. Tom refused, saying he couldn't do it. Legree beat Tom savagely trying to break his will. He told Tom, "Ain't you mine now, body and soul?" With tears and blood flowing down his face, Tom replied, "My soul ain't yours. You haven't bought it, Mas'r, and you can't buy it. It's been bought and paid for by One who is able to keep it. You can't harm me." Eventually Legree had Tom beaten to death after two other slaves escaped, but his faith never wavered.

Today calling someone an "Uncle Tom" is an insult, but that is based on a misunderstanding of the original meaning of the book. Rather than being too subservient, Tom is too Christian for modern thinking. He suffered patiently, just as Peter instructed believers to do. When we endure reproach for the sake of Christ, we will receive eternal rewards.

THIRTEEN

Who Will Harm You?

And who is he that will harm you, if ye be followers of that which is
good? But and if ye suffer for righteousness' sake, happy are ye: and
be not afraid of their terror, neither be troubled; But sanctify the
Lord God in your hearts: and be ready always to give an answer to
every man that asketh you a reason of the hope that is in you with
meekness and fear: Having a good conscience; that, whereas they
speak evil of you, as of evildoers, they may be ashamed that falsely
accuse your good conversation in Christ. For it is better, if the
will of God be so, that ye suffer for well doing, than for evil doing.
—1 Peter 3:13–17

At first glance it seems as though verse 13 and verse 14 contradict each other. The concept of no one harming you is followed by the reality of suffering for the sake of righteousness.

To properly interpret these two verses, we need to take a long term view. In the long term, no one can harm you. Your salvation was purchased by the blood of Christ, and no one can take you out of His hand. You are secure. Nothing anyone does can change your ultimate destiny. Along the way, however, you may suffer for doing what is right.

Many popular preachers today are broadcasting a message that if you have enough faith, everything will be wonderful. You will be in great health, you will enjoy only prosperity, your life will be filled with good things, and all your children will be above average. That's not what the Bible says. The Bible gives us full and fair warning to expect trouble as a part of life.

The man that the Spirit of God inspired to write these words was Peter. When this epistle was written, Nero ruled in Rome. He was an incredibly wicked man. He delighted in persecuting Christians. He forced them to face lions in the Coliseum. He tied them to stakes and lit them on fire to light his garden parties at night. He murdered thousands for their faith, and he was ultimately responsible for Peter's death. The concept of suffering was not academic for Peter; it was a daily reality.

In addition to that, Peter knew that he would die as a martyr because Jesus told him that by the Sea of Galilee (John 21:18–19). He had been in jail at least twice and sentenced to death once, but an angel delivered him (Acts 12:1–11). Peter's concept of suffering wasn't having his feelings hurt by someone saying something mean; it was the threat of physical pain and even death. Sometimes we act as though we are the first Christians to "suffer for Jesus," but the history of the church is a history of persecuted martyrs who were faithful unto death. Peter gives us three important principles to consider when we are facing hard times.

THE REALITY

We are promised ultimate protection. No one can change your eternal destination, but you may have some bumps in the road on the journey. I'm not a big fan of traffic jams. It seems as though every road between Bridgeport and Saginaw is under construction at the same time. We may have to make detours. We may even take wrong turns. Our ultimate destination, however, is secure.

We are guaranteed unavoidable problems. Jesus promised, *"In this world ye shall have tribulation"* (John 16:33). Attacks will come. Things will happen that we don't like. If you listen to some preachers on television (you shouldn't), you would think that everything in life will be perfect and you will never stub your toe on a door frame and get a hangnail. That's not reality.

We are offered unbelievable peace. Have you ever suffered and been happy about it? That's not the normal response to say the least. Yet the Bible says that we are "happy" or "blessed" when we suffer for righteousness. This is not the happiness that means "to be delighted"; it is the happiness that means "to be highly privileged." In Philippians 1:29 Paul said, *"For unto you it is given in the behalf of Christ, not only to believe on him, but also to suffer for his sake."* The word translated *given* there comes from the Greek root word *charis*—the word for grace. Suffering is a gift from God in the same way salvation is. It is a privilege. It is in the midst of our suffering that we experience His comfort and peace as never before.

THE RESPONSE

When we are going through difficulties and suffering, we must not give in to fear. Fear is a natural response, but it is a wrong response. Peter said, *"be not afraid of their terror"* (1 Peter 3:14). That means that even when they try to terrify us, we should not be fearful. If the enemy can use fear and intimidation to keep you from doing right, he wins. Fear is a powerful weapon, but it only works if you allow it to work.

Over the last decade or so we've become very familiar with the concept of terrorism. The purpose of the terrorist is to terrify people into changing their behavior. If you lined up all of the members of Al Qaeda and the other organizations attacking US military personnel out in the open, they wouldn't last one day. They rely on fear to do their work for them. In the same way, though our enemies cannot defeat us, they can use fear to keep us from doing what we should for God. Do what is right no matter what forces are arrayed against you.

We are also told to *"sanctify the Lord God in* [our] *hearts"* (1 Peter 3:15). To *sanctify* means "to set apart." Trouble should increase our consecration. This phrase Peter uses actually comes from a story found in the book of Isaiah. During this particular time in Isaiah's ministry, Ahaz was the king of Judah. Syria had joined with the Northern Kingdom of Israel to attack him. Ahaz decided to bribe the Assyrians to help him. In Isaiah chapter 7, Isaiah goes to Ahaz to offer him something better than a heathen king with his army—the help of Almighty God.

Isaiah 8:13 says, *"Sanctify the LORD of hosts himself; and let him be your fear, and let him be your dread."* What Isaiah was telling the king and the people of Judah (and us) is that our confidence should be in no one else but God and that we should fear no one else but Him. Ahaz was facing a difficult situation, but joining forces with the ungodly is never the solution. Instead of being afraid of his enemies, Ahaz needed to fear God. When we put Him in first place, sanctifying Him in our hearts, He works on our behalf.

Ahaz did not listen to Isaiah. He went ahead and partnered with the Assyrians. They fought together and defeated Syria. His plan was great. Everything worked just the way Ahaz wanted it to work. But then Ahaz died. His son was Hezekiah who grew up to be a good king, probably the best God's people had except for David. However, he spent much of his reign fighting off the attacks of one particular enemy—the Assyrians. When you partner with the world to fight your enemies, as Ahaz did, their appetite may not be satisfied. They may come and devour you next. You may survive, but you may be setting up a problem for your children and future generations.

You should be more worried about displeasing God than anything your enemies say or do. Peter here repeats the warning Isaiah gave to Ahaz to remind us of this vital truth. Nothing your enemies do can stop you from accomplishing God's purpose— only you can do that. Don't let fearing anything or anyone keep you from fearing God and doing His will. If you please God, everything else will take care of itself.

Scared people usually aren't focused on pleasing God. Worried people usually aren't thinking about pleasing God. They are looking out for themselves. Faith looks to God and trusts whatever He provides. When things get tough, we need to make a conscious effort to say, "God, what do You want me to do? What is the right thing to do? How can I best please and bring glory to You?"

THE READINESS

Dealing with trouble often gives you an opportunity to witness. That's why Peter reminds us of the importance of being *"ready always to give an answer"* (1 Peter 3:15). As a man introduced me to preach once, he said, "I don't think I've ever asked Brother Ouellette a question when he didn't give me a Bible verse for an answer." I don't believe that his statement was completely accurate, but I want it to be. I want my mind to be filled with and controlled by the Word of God so that I'm always ready with His answer instead of my own wisdom. I want my principles and my answers to others to be based on Scripture.

The concept of being ready is the idea of being prepared. The motto of the Coast Guard is *semper paratus*—"always ready." As you go through times of trouble, think about how you can respond if you are asked for the reasons of your faith. If we spent more time focused on Him in our trials rather than griping and complaining, we might find more people asking us those kinds of questions. The word used here for answer is the Greek word from which we get our word *apologetics*—the formal defense of the faith. It's important not only to believe the right thing but also to know why you believe the right thing.

Even in troubled times we still have hope. When Peter talks about the *"hope that is in us,"* he is not referring to a wish that things would somehow work out; rather he is talking about something we anticipate with pleasure. When you obey God, you can look forward confidently to the day when things work out for your best.

Isaiah 46:9–10 says, *"Remember the former things of old: for I am God, and there is none else; I am God, and there is none like me, Declaring the end from the beginning, and from ancient times the things that are not yet done, saying, My counsel shall stand, and I will do all my pleasure."* The things that God has planned that haven't happened yet are just as sure and certain as those that already have. He will do all that He purposes to do. You can count on it. Don't be timid; be confident. You can "what if" yourself into a nervous breakdown. The same God who fed the Israelites in the wilderness for forty years can feed you today.

Notice that we are to respond to others with meekness. A gentle spirit and a good attitude are attractive. Our confidence is not in ourselves; it is in God. We should not be arrogant or offensive. Being a jerk is not a very productive evangelistic technique. Tell the truth without apology, but show kindness while you do it.

THE RESULTS

What happens if we sanctify the Lord God in our hearts? What happens if we decide we are not going to be afraid of terror? What happens if we respond to suffering in faith rather than in fear? It will produce some wonderful results in our lives.

First, we see that we will have a clear conscience. I want to have a good reputation. It's important to me to maintain my testimony for the Lord. But it's far more important that I be right on the inside. I do not want anything in my life that is unresolved and keeps weighing on my conscience. Paul said, *"I exercise myself, to have always a conscience void of offence toward God, and toward men"* (Acts 24:16).

I heard about a farmer who hired a handyman to help him. When the farmer asked if the man would work hard he replied, "I sleep well at night." Then he asked, "Can I trust you?" and again the man replied, "I sleep well at night." After the new man had been there a few days, there was a huge storm in the middle of the night. The farmer thought he had better check to see if everything was okay. He found the barn shut up tight, the gates closed and locked, and all the animals safe in their pens. The next morning he went to see the hired man. "I see you did all the chores before you went to bed," he said. "I told you I sleep well at night," the man replied. He slept well because his conscience was clear—he knew he had done what he was supposed to do. A clear conscience is a blessing.

Second, we see that we will have a good conversation. The idea here is the same one found in Titus 2:7 where it talks about having a *"pattern of good works."* The concept is of a blueprint, a pattern to follow to obtain the desired results. In other words, our lives are to be an example that others can follow. This kind of life is not created by the power of the flesh; it only happens through the power of the Spirit of God.

Though such a life is our goal, it does not carry a guarantee that no one will critique us—they criticized Jesus, calling Him a drunkard and a glutton. It means that they will have no legitimate grounds for their complaint. We got an email the other day from a lady who was upset because people from our church kept coming by and witnessing to her and leaving tracts at her house. She had lived at several different addresses in our town, and apparently we found her at every one! She could and did complain, but she had no grounds to accuse us of doing wrong. It's far better to suffer for doing right rather than for doing wrong.

I got a phone call from a pastor who was very upset about things people were saying about him. He said, "Brother Ouellette, they keep saying these things about me, and they just aren't true." I said, "Good. I'd rather be lied about than have what they say to be true." I tried to encourage him and help him. Realize this: part of being like Jesus is being falsely accused and even suffering. First Peter 2:21 says, *"Christ also suffered for us, leaving us an example, that ye should follow his steps."* Though He went to the cross and suffered and died, He was not harmed. He accomplished God's purpose, and if you sanctify God in your heart, nothing that anyone else does to you can do anything except accomplish His plan for your life.

FOURTEEN

Let Not Your Heart Be Troubled

Let not your heart be troubled: ye believe in God, believe also in me. In my Father's house are many mansions: if it were not so, I would have told you. I go to prepare a place for you. And if I go and prepare a place for you, I will come again, and receive you unto myself; that where I am, there ye may be also. And whither I go ye know, and the way ye know. Thomas saith unto him, Lord, we know not whither thou goest; and how can we know the way? Jesus saith unto him, I am the way, the truth, and the life: no man cometh unto the Father, but by me. If ye had known me, ye should have known my Father also: and from henceforth ye know him, and have seen him. Philip saith unto him, Lord, shew us the Father, and it sufficeth us. Jesus saith unto him, Have I been so long time with you, and yet hast thou not known me, Philip? he that hath seen me hath seen the Father; and how sayest thou then, Shew us the Father? Believest thou not that I am in the Father, and the Father in me? the words that I speak unto you I speak not of myself: but the Father that dwelleth in me, he doeth the works. Believe me that I am in the Father, and the Father in me: or else believe me for the very works' sake. Verily, verily, I say unto you, He that believeth on me, the works that I do shall he do also; and greater works than these shall he do; because I go unto my Father. And whatsoever ye shall ask in my name, that will I do, that the Father may be glorified in the Son. If ye shall ask any thing in my name, I will do it.—JOHN 14:1–14

This passage is found in the account of the Last Supper, the final evening Jesus spent with His disciples before His crucifixion. They had followed Him for three years and watched Him heal, teach, pray for, and minister to people in need. Now they are about to watch Him die, and they are not ready. In fact, there is a great deal of confusion and concern. After the meal was over, Jesus took water and washed the disciples' feet.

As Jesus spoke, He was preparing them for more than just His death; He was preparing them for a great transition. No longer would they have the Lord walking with them in human form. Now they would receive the indwelling Holy Spirit to guide and empower them as they took the Gospel around the world. The old covenant was ending, and a new one was taking its place. Jesus prepared the disciples by making a series of promises to them—promises that were meant to help them and us to endure the troubled times that were and are to come.

JESUS PROMISED A NEW PEACE

Jesus said, *"Let not your heart be troubled: ye believe in God, believe also in me."* Most of the time we think of peace as something that just happens, but the point Jesus makes here is that peace is a result of not allowing our hearts to be captured by fear and worry. It's easy to have peace when you have paid bills, a healthy family, a running car, and a good job. Peace is not an external force that descends on some people through a mysterious process; peace is an internal result of our choices and actions.

It is natural for our hearts to be troubled; that is a tendency that comes with living in a fallen world. Situations in life may trouble you, but they don't have to if you don't let them. The word *troubled* here means "stirred up or agitated." In some washing machines, there is an agitator. Its job is to keep the clothes moving so they can get clean. If the clothes had peace, they wouldn't wash well. This world is filled with agitators, but they should not control us or our responses.

Philippians 4:6 says, *"Be careful* [filled with anxiety] *for nothing; but in every thing by prayer and supplication with thanksgiving let your requests be made known unto God."* I think the element of thanksgiving is what we are often missing from our prayers. We are not just to pour out our troubles before the Lord; we are also to thank Him. That is the kind of praying that leads to the *"peace of God, which passeth all understanding"* (Philippians 4:7).

We often skip the next step. If our hearts are not to be troubled, we also must control our thinking. *"Think on these things"* (Philippians 4:8) means to focus our thoughts on the right things. This world will give you plenty of input that leads to fear, anxiety, distress, and worry, but you don't have to think on those things. If you want to control your heart, you must first control what goes into it.

JESUS PROMISED A NEW PLACE

Jesus said, *"I go to prepare a place for you."* Jesus told His disciples that there were "many mansions" in His Father's house. The word for *many* here indicates an abundance; it's the word used to describe the longest numbers. I don't know how many people will be in Heaven, but there will be a place for all of them. The word *mansion* in modern English conveys the idea of a big fancy house, but the underlying Greek word is even more than that. It talks about a permanent residence, a dwelling place for us forever.

I don't know that there is actual building work going on in Heaven. Everything in our world was spoken into existence by God in just six days. Now nearly two thousand years have passed. The Bible doesn't tell us any more about this preparation process, but if the incredible beauty of our natural world took just a few days, how wonderful will Heaven be? I also know that Jesus was a carpenter, and I'm pretty sure that any place He prepares for us will be absolutely perfect.

Heaven is a real place. Many years ago, Dr. John R. Rice wrote a book called *Bible Facts about Heaven* and sent it off to be published. When the manuscript came back from the editor, they had gone through and replaced the capital *H* with a small *h* every time he referred to Heaven. They said, "It's not grammatically correct to capitalize Heaven." Dr. Rice said, "Do you capitalize Chicago?" They said, "Of course, it's a real place." Dr. Rice said, "So is Heaven." And it is real.

Heaven is also for us. Jesus not only promised to prepare the place, but He promised to return and take us to it. Many people espouse an end-times view called post-millennialism—the notion that we must work to bring about the Kingdom of God on Earth. They believe that if we work hard enough and long enough and get enough people saved, the Lord will return. Some good men have believed and taught that, but it doesn't match what Jesus said. He is going to return in order to fix things, not after we fix things. The return of Jesus is the blessed hope of every believer, and it is an assurance against our hearts being troubled when times are hard.

It is just as certain that Jesus will return for us as it is that He came the first time. Our choir sings a song sometimes that says, "He went away, but not to stay." The disciples didn't really understand what Jesus was telling them. They were focused on the present. They expected Jesus to overthrow the Romans and set up His kingdom on Earth right then. The idea that He was going away to prepare a place wasn't what they were seeking. Jesus could have berated them for not understanding what He had been teaching them, but instead He made this wonderful statement: *"I am the way, the truth, and the life."*

Everything in our lives is about Jesus. The only way we can be saved is by grace through faith in Him. The only way we can be sanctified as we walk through this world is by following His way. The only way we can reach Heaven is through Him. Dr. Bob Jones, Sr. told the story of a testimony time he had in one of his meetings. An old preacher stood and said in a frail voice, "My wife is gone. My family is gone. I'm old, and I can't preach any more. All I have is Jesus." He sat back down, and others gave their testimonies. Then the old preacher stood back up and said, "Dr. Bob, all I need is Jesus."

I don't mean to minimize your problems in any way. I know there are real hurts and real pains and real pressures in your life. I know the bank may be about to repossess the house, and the doctor may have given you a bad report. The boss may have warned you to expect to be laid off, and you may be having trouble with your children. But listen: If you have Jesus, you have all you need. He is the way.

It's interesting to me that Philip asked to see the Father. He said, "If we could just see the Father, we would be satisfied." But God is a spirit, and the only way we can worship Him is not to see Him but to have faith and worship Him in spirit and truth. Jesus responded with a great doctrinal truth—if we have seen Him, we have already seen the Father. They are one. Then Jesus reiterates the vital importance of faith. He says to Philip, "Believe me." When push comes to shove, when the troubled times come, do you believe God or not? If you do, your heart will not be troubled, no matter what else happens.

JESUS PROMISED A NEW PRODUCTIVITY

Jesus said, *"He that believeth on me, the works that I do shall he do also; and greater works than these shall he do; because I go unto my Father"* (John 14:12). Sometimes we get so familiar with the Bible that we don't pay attention to what it actually says. This is a staggering statement. The Lord Jesus went about healing all those who were sick. He made the blind see, the deaf hear and the lame walk. He even raised the dead. If we are going to do greater works, that's pretty amazing. What did Jesus mean?

The works that Jesus did were miraculous, but they were temporal. The thousands of people who were fed from one little boy's lunch got hungry again. Lazarus was raised from the dead, but he's not still alive today. Jesus said we would do greater works because He was leaving to return to the Father. When Jesus left, He sent the Holy Spirit. Though He was God, Jesus lived in a man's body, which meant He was, in a sense, limited to being in one place at a time. The Holy Spirit indwells us wherever we are and is present in all believers at once. We can do great works because we have been given great power.

If you think about it, the disciples were an unlikely group of men to choose to change the world. Peter was impetuous and unfaithful; Thomas was a doubter; James and John wanted to call down fire from Heaven to destroy those who wouldn't listen.

Matthew had been a collaborator with the Romans in their tax schemes; Philip didn't recognize Jesus' relationship with His Father, and Simon Zelotes may well have been involved in violent attempts to overthrow the Roman occupation of Israel. If they were going to do great works, it wasn't going to be in their own strength and ability. In the same way, if you are going to be productive for God and overcome troubled times, it will not be your doing.

I was in the airport not long ago and needed to get my shoes shined. The man who did it was visibly upset. I tried to talk to him to find out what was going on, but he wasn't very talkative. I asked, "You're having a hard time, aren't you?" In response he began to cry. Because he wouldn't talk, I gave him a tract and a good tip and said, "Here's something to encourage you." I don't know if he will respond to the Gospel message I left with him or not. Not every door I push on opens, but none of the doors I don't push will open. You can be productive for God no matter what else is going on in your life.

JESUS PROMISED A NEW PROVISION

Jesus said, *"If ye shall ask anything in my name, I will do it."* Notice carefully that Jesus does not say we can ask for anything we want and get it; rather He says we will receive what we ask for in His name. What does it mean to ask for something in the name of Jesus? It is not tacking the words "in Jesus' name" on the end of a prayer. Instead, praying in Jesus' name means we are praying in His authority.

We have several police officers in our church. If one of them walked out into traffic in his church clothes and said "Stop," people would keep going. However, let him put on his uniform, and the situation changes. Now he has authority. It is not the person but the position he fills that conveys the authority. His authority is given by the law. A policeman doesn't have the right to stop you because he doesn't like the color or make of the car you're driving. However, if you're going twenty miles an hour over the speed limit, he has every right to pull you over.

When I pray in Jesus' name, I am praying within the boundaries of His will. I am not asking for things that are contrary to His character and His commands. It's not possible to receive things in Jesus' name that would dishonor that name. If you are praying for things that advance the Kingdom of God and bring glory to the name of Jesus, you can be confident of receiving the answer you need.

Let me apply this teaching on prayer specifically for people in troubled times. If you are praying for a way out of the trouble in which you find yourself, you are doing what you should do. You should keep praying until either you get the answer you need or God changes your prayer. It's important to remember that we don't always know what is best for us. The Apostle Paul found himself in that position. He was suffering a debilitating physical ailment, and he prayed fervently and repeatedly for it to go away.

And lest I should be exalted above measure through the abundance of the revelations, there was given to me a thorn in the flesh, the messenger of Satan to buffet me, lest I should be exalted above measure. For this thing I besought the Lord thrice, that it might depart from me. And he said unto me, My grace is sufficient for thee: for my strength is made perfect in weakness. Most gladly therefore will I rather glory in my infirmities, that the power of Christ may rest upon me. Therefore I take pleasure in infirmities, in reproaches, in necessities, in persecutions, in distresses for Christ's sake: for when I am weak, then am I strong.—2 CORINTHIANS 12:7–10*

If God does not answer your prayer as you expect, consider that the problem you are experiencing may be for His glory and for your good. If you are not delivered from your troubles, you can still be delivered in them. Rest in God's grace and allow it to be sufficient for whatever you need. Be willing to change your prayers and accept God's answer.

JESUS PROMISED A NEW PARTNER

Jesus said, *"I will pray the Father, and he shall give you another Comforter"* (John 14:16). As you read the Bible you see that the Holy Spirit has always worked among God's people. Old Testament believers did receive His power. He came upon Samson and made possible his great feats of strength. He spoke to prophets such as Elijah and Elisha and equipped them to do miraculous things. However, His presence was not a permanent presence. Now the relationship between God's people and the Holy Spirit was about to change. Jesus said that from that point on, the Holy Spirit would *"abide with you for ever."*

At the moment you were saved, the Holy Spirit came to indwell your heart, and He came to stay. The Holy Spirit is just as much God as the Father and the Son. Some people talk about Him as though He is an impersonal force, but He is far more than that. As we saw earlier, Jesus was in one place at a time during His earthly ministry, but the Holy Spirit is present with all believers everywhere in the world.

Not every believer walks in the Spirit and not every believer is filled with the Spirit, but every believer has the Holy Spirit as a real presence in his life. What is the purpose of this new partner that Jesus promised? First Corinthians 12:11 tells us that the Holy Spirit provides us with different gifts to be used in building the body of Christ. Certain sign gifts operated during the early church, but these were temporary. They are not meant for today. But there are also service gifts—helps, administration, mercy, teaching, giving, and more—that are vital to the growth and health of the church today.

You have one or more of these gifts, and you should be using what God has given you. I've found that sometimes people claim they don't have the gift of doing something they don't want to do. You are supposed to do right and obey God even in areas where you aren't particularly gifted. Everyone is supposed to give tithes and offerings; some people have a special gift to do more giving. Everyone is supposed to show love and compassion to those who are hurting; some people have a special gift of mercy.

The Holy Spirit also produces fruit in our lives. Galatians 5:22–23 says, *"But the fruit of the Spirit is love, joy, peace, longsuffering, gentleness, goodness, faith, Meekness, temperance: against such there is no law."* Some people treat this as a checklist of different qualities and character traits, but actually only one fruit of the Spirit has these different manifestations. In light of our focus on troubled times, I want to call your special attention to the fruit of peace.

This peace is not something we create—it is His fruit. No matter what my circumstances, I can have peace if I am yielded to His control. I don't produce it in my own power, wisdom, strength, or self-control. Jesus promised His disciples, and us, that the Holy Spirit, our new partner, would come into our lives and keep our hearts from being troubled regardless of what comes into our lives. No trouble you ever face will break His promises to you or remove the presence of the Holy Spirit from your life.

Jesus did not promise that we would never go through trying and difficult times; instead He promised His Spirit to bring us comfort, help, strength, and encouragement so that no matter what happens, our hearts will not be troubled. God's peace is available to you in this world for the trying times you experience, and even better, we have the wonderful and certain promise of spending eternity with Him in Heaven to look forward to. When you are tempted to be overcome with worry, when your heart is troubled, when you don't see a way out—look up! *"This same Jesus, which is taken up from you into heaven, shall so come in like manner as ye have seen him go into heaven"* (Acts 1:11). *"And so shall we ever be with the Lord"* (1 Thessalonians 4:17).

Conclusion

A little girl whose father captained a large ship pleaded with her father that he would take her on one of his journeys. After he agreed, he selected a trip that would not be unusually long in duration and during which he expected no difficult seas.

Contrary to his expectations, a terrible storm suddenly arose. The winds blew fiercely, cold waves crashed over the sides of the ship, and gigantic raindrops pounded the vessel and its occupants. The ship bounced up and down on the troubled ocean. Flashes of lightning revealed looks of concern on the faces of even the most seasoned of seamen. One sailor went to where the little girl was huddled in a corner of the wheelhouse and asked if she was all right. "Oh," she smiled. "I'm fine. When the lightning flashed a moment ago, I saw my daddy. He's at the wheel, so everything will be all right."

How true are the words of the Sunday school song I was taught so many years ago: "With Christ in the vessel, we can smile at the storm...." No matter how troubled the times, the Spirit-led, surrendered child of God can rest in the truth that "My Father is at the wheel."

Visit us online

strivingtogether.com

wcbc.edu

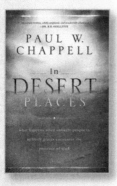

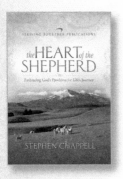